FROM INSIDE THE BEAST

100 Prison Poems and Appropriations

---

by Lawrence B. Salander

Inmate: 10a5186
Cell 35 Unit 10-2
Midstate Correctional Facility
Marcy, New York

AUSTIN MACAULEY PUBLISHERS™
LONDON • CAMBRIDGE • NEW YORK • SHARJAH

Copyright © Lawrence B. Salander 2022

The right of Lawrence B. Salander to be identified as author of this work has been asserted in accordance with section 77 and 78 of the Copyright, Designs and Patents Act 1988.

All rights reserved. No part of this publication may be reproduced, stored in a retrieval system, or transmitted in any form or by any means, electronic, mechanical, photocopying, recording, or otherwise, without the prior permission of the publishers.

Any person who commits any unauthorised act in relation to this publication may be liable to criminal prosecution and civil claims for damages.

A CIP catalogue record for this title is available from the British Library.

ISBN 9781528966665 (Paperback)
ISBN 9781528968850 (ePub e-book)

www.austinmacauley.com

First Published 2022
Austin Macauley Publishers Ltd®
1 Canada Square
Canary Wharf
London
E14 5AA

But my mind clung to my wife's image, imagining it with an uncanny acuteness. I heard her answering, I saw her smile, her frank encouraging look. Real or not, her look was more luminous than the sun, which was beginning to rise.

A thought transfixed me......... The truth----that love is the ultimate and the highest goal to which man can aspire......... The salvation of man is through love and in love. I understood how a man who has nothing left in the world can still know bliss, be it only for a brief moment, in the contemplation of his beloved. In a position of utter desolation, when man cannot express himself in positive action, when his only achievement may consist in enduring his sufferings in the right way---an honorable way---in such a position man can, through the loving contemplation of the image he carries of his beloved, achieve fulfillment.

                Viktor Frankl, *Man's Search for Meaning* (Beacon Press)

POEMS

Autobiography   7
Again (Stonington)   10
My Angel of San Rocco   12
Joyce in Zurich   14
You and Me (A Love Poem)   16
The Hounds of Shame   18
Signs   20
The Child of the Sacred Cow   23
Drowned   24
A Walk and After   26
Apology   30
Irony   33
Better Days   35
The Devil's Dance   38
Odyssey   40
A Pair of Sins   43
Memorial   44
Like Jojo Last Monday (Through Melville's Eyes)   47
Black Stockings   49
Lost   52
Love Poem   54
Summer Music   56
The Lunatic's Rodeo   58
Hammer   60
Ahab's Boat   62
Trio   64
Unsettled Time   66
Vapors and Starry Beasts   68
Ambiguities   70
Death the Dancer   73
A Million Ways   76
Neptunia   78
Contradictions   80

Clowns   85
Moon Howling   88
The Courage It Takes   91
High Stakes and Hurricanes   92
Wild Rice and Cornish Hens   94
No More Talk   97
Whale Hunter   100
Ecce Homo   101
Once Upon a Time and Then (Honeymoon)   105
When the Howling Stops   107
The Color of the Stars   109
The Inheritance   111
Mystery Road   114
Last Nights   116
October's Page (The Calendar)   119
Bad Dreams and Good   120
Hosana on the Day   124
Donahue's   126
Cold Suns and Rainless Clouds   128
Misplaced   130
The Ballad of Joe Smith   132
Revolution Time   136
After All   141
Speaking of the Soul   143
The Lie   146
The Holy Train   149
Prehistoria   154
Silent Flashes   156
Doubled Down   158
King   159
Dance   161
Home (For Richie)   164
Mystic Doors   166

Ringmaster　168
Animals　172
Bewildered and Repelled　173
The Price Paid to Sing　176
Brahma Bull Bat Outta Hell　179
Tests　181
Flipside　184
Gauzy　187
Pings　189
Eve and Adam　192
Sacrament?　197
Ciborium　204
Prayer　206
Father Friend　209
The Great Deflation　212
Awfully Close　217
Affirmations　221

Tantrum　224
A Bigger Thing　225
A Certain Satisfaction　230
Blood and Tears　233
Changing States　237
Serial Sinner　241
Quarantine　244
Once a Day　248
Easier Said Than Done　250
The City　253
Well Rehearsed　255
Tears of Blood　258
Before the Slaughter　262
Saint Vitus' Dancers　271
Shards　275
Blighted Hopes　278
de Rigueur　283

For all my children and Layla and for what once was between the woman with the green benotched Kentucky Irish eyes and the author of these poems.

AUTOBIOGRAPHY

The wild waters
Spoke in frenzied sounds
The thunder about a mile away
Barrel staves from the bayside
Broke through the Beach
Finally free
When the water and the wind
Swept the sand away

Then the rain soaked the sand to mud
The changing tides
Became the ocean's floor again
Beneath the breaking water mountains
And the white noise they made

Then the wind
Made a mad music of its own
And the clouds cleared
The sultry sun

God's great glory

That's love
That's all anyone
Should ever need

And the cyclonic wonder waves
And the color of The Lord's luminosities
Could not compare
To the beauty of you
My eyes drank their fill there

And all that fantastic fertile feeling
And all those starry water skies
Shined
In your notched green Kentucky Irish eyes
In the silent songs they whispered
To my breathless heart

All this the sound and color
Of your love sonata

Before
In that place of my younger years
I sang sweet songs of home
At the wind
And the wild water

Searching and yearning
I learned to dream there
With my then free heart
And unscarred soul

There
Dreams were not pictures
And never stories
They were experience

I ate the color there
Imbibed the salty air
Inebriated
My senses were on overload

Now the prestidigitators play the magic men
To awe and make us wonder
Like they were false gods
Who make men mad
And mothers crazy

The wealth weary worldly ones
The worthless and the fat
The dissipated die
Their loveless souls lie still
In the deepest darkest place
In Hell

Winter chilled bones in fiery places
Glimpses of others' joy
But in here there's only howling
And the irony which is the fate
Of the sated lustful money whores

All of whom leave this world penniless
Encased in bronze against the worms
That will have their way with them
Anyway

Money mad and puny
Desperate kings
And the sycophantic fucks who adore them
Disappear
Like David's grassy place
When the wind
Blows over their blasted bones
And gnashed broken teeth

They are remembered not

The savage storms
Blew your sweet soul to me
Hopelessly lost
In the love we made

When I die
My love
Bury me
On that year's bloody beach
Or cast me out to sea
Filled up with the love of you

Without you
Was the death of me.

2012 / 2017 / 2020 / 2021 / 2022

AGAIN (STONINGTON)

Hellhounds howl
Lunatics laugh in a sea of blood
And the grotesque party hard
As Satan's Soldiers stoke the fires
Of outrageousness and insanity
For those of us who dwell here in Hell

Satan's sounds
Carry across the starry spaces
Heard only by the few
Deranged enough to hear
Like some kind of primal knowledge
Or instinct
That comes with low intentions

My own war waged
In the dark places
Of my solitary soul
For I am alone
And scared shitless too
So I listen to the party music
The Devil spins

Maniacs slaughter children
With weapons profit born
And the fat cat chiefs celebrate
The bloated bottom line
All the time pretending
To mourn the massacre
From which they gained so much

For the killing of the innocent
Sorry is not good enough
An eye for and eye a tooth for a tooth
We turn to God to understand
They worship their own of green paper

Enlistees console sit
Sweaty palms stroke their sticks of joy
Drone pilots maneuvering
Without learning how to fly
Inglorious and ignorant
They follow the orders
Of evil old men
Who fight for profit only

In the name of God
And their now failed country

Corrupted and putrefied
The way they see it
Money is the only sacred thing

Coin lust
Twenty-four seven news
Profits made in babies' blood
They make killings in the slaughterings

The masses blame the crazy ones
Purposely distracted
And as long as we permit it
The good die young again

The rich men sup
With golden spoons
Sleep
On Satan's satin sheets

2012 / 2017 / 2020 / 2021 / 2022

MY ANGEL OF SAN ROCCO

The angel in Robusti's place
Was mine that day in Venice
Silver November light
Framed her shadow
Bundled against the Scuola's numbing cold

Her stocking hat
Her coat and my own
Her leaky nose
Watching as I looked

She took my breath away
Sitting where the Caracci sat
Seeing what they saw
While I played
In Tintoretto's spaces

That kind of love can kill
The one left loving in the end
An agonizing death
The pain never ceases
Until oblivion of course

There was a howling then
Like the night of the Machamuvous
The night He killed Egypt's first born
The way it always is
When the Reaper is around
Reaping

Misplaced remorse
Ill - considered pain
There are many things in living worse than death
Like that
Like this

O but to have lived and so loved
That glorious day
An angel in a fairytale
A wonderful water world
The love we shared and made
Worth the pain in living now without you

2012 / 2017 / 2020 / 2021 / 2022

JOYCE IN ZURICH

The great man's coat kept the cold at bay
Like the sky
An icy inglorious gray
His heart froze hard for his daughter's pain
He begged God to make his own instead

As he sat and cried as fathers will
In the snow
And in the freezing rain

Money won't
Bring my daughter back
Nor can it make her well
What is art in the face of life
When she lives in Hell?

Fuck all my genius
It's only art is all
My wife cried herself to sleep again
In our bed near the pitted wall

I would talk to God
If I remembered how
Beg and pray and plead
But too many years have come and gone
Since I was last on bended knee

A long way from the sacristy
A long time since a choir boy
No longer a young artist
No longer a Dubliner
Ulysses travels 'round the known world
I am stuck here in guilt
And a father's love for a hurting child

My life
My art
My soul
Mean nothing now
Nothing much at all if they ever did
When it was warm
Before the fall
Before we came to Zurich

2012 / 2017 / 2020 / 2021 / 2022

YOU AND ME (A LOVE POEM)

When first we met the chemistry
Instantly we knew
You couldn't get enough of me
Nor I enough of you
The heat was high between us
It happens to so few
A hearty vital lusty love
Long after it was new

A unity
A give and take
When we were making love
So tangled up together
I could barely see
Which part of us was you
Which part of us was me

But it was never just the joining
The merger of we two
You were
You are my angel
And you will always be
Stripped of all
In this horrid Hell
Holding hard onto our history

And the four of them
And their own will prove
That which was once true
The bonding of two hearts and souls
The love of me and you

Do you hear it my love ?
Through the pouring rain
That noise that speaks of hurting
My excruciating pain
The sound of a broken heart
The never-ending strife
The necessary unburdening
Of what passes for my life

When we were together
I often was confused
I hate the part of us was me

And love the part was you
I'll live until I lose the dream
Of you and me my all
Of loving like we used to love
In the time before the fall

We can never know the future
It's some kind of mystery
But I know the way it was
How well we loved
In the time we spent together
The time of you and me

2012 / 2017 / 2020 / 2021 / 2022

THE HOUNDS OF SHAME

The flattery of royalty
Tried the music in Mozart's head
Diminished by the compromise
In fitting in with mortal man
In writing the music down
In a form
Musicians were able to play
Divinity was set aside for compromise

I wish
I could hear the music
As it was
In Mozart's head

Fat fucks
Still feed their savage souls
But the beauty still exists

Broken by life's lost loves
Beggars bay like I do
With the other hounds of shame

The white moon casts blue shadows here
The Godly sing hallelujah
The damned die dirty deaths

Heaven was where we lived
And Hell is anywhere without you

Once we dwelt in that gorgeous garden
Where the original you
And I
The first lovesick me
Lived for a while
Expelled for lusting
Looking to an envious world
Like we had too much
But now there is no we
And we have nothing

The lunatics and I howled hard tonight
For the sum of all lost love
Which made them and this foundering fool
Crazy in the first place

2012 / 2017 / 2020 / 2021 / 2022

SIGNS

I fought the fight on Heaven's plains
But lost the war in Hell
My soul sick heart destroyed
No one to ease the pain in here
The sun has broken open
The most evil of our evil days

The pit in which I lay dug deep
In the smoldering dirt
In this hot place it's freezing cold
I am lost in agony
It's hard to think
Of anything but pain
Exactly what damnation's for

The site of my devastation
There is no coming back from there
A broken hearted desolation
There are no resurrected souls in here

If I'm ever free again
Best leave me to myself and those I love

Don't fuck with me
Don't try to stifle my rage
I'm ready for The Reaper-Man

When Death arrives
No matter what my age
Death holds no fear for men like me
So well schooled in misery

The canyons lined with sandstone tombs
Vultures circle the sky
Coyotes howl the western moon
Desert flower soliloquies

There is a roiling in the Universe
Satan is set to play
Beauty fades to darkness
Judgment Day

The levitating moon hangs upside down
Savage souls and heavy hearts rule the day
In constant pain and ugly rage
O let the damned devil's roar!

When false prophets party
It's madness and idolatry
Let the angels fly away

Alienated souls make no amends
For they will spend forever
In that place of woe
They have nothing more to lose
Like an inmate facing life in jail
Dangerous

Darkened suns
Chariots of fire fill the skies
Lightning rips the heavens wide
Striking Buonarroti's dome
Still Saint Peter sleeps

Meteors end their cosmic light year trips
Crash into Russia's Steppes
And the Holy Land's in revolution
Near the plains of Armageddon

The sack clothed sun still warms the holy ones
The seas run red
With first-born's blood
Once complacent songs
Now songs of shame

The remorseful run from their desire
Though they've already lost it in their hearts
Far too little
Far too late

Now consigned to Satan's fire
The signs are clear
The end is near
We've been waiting two thousand twenty years
For the coming of The Lord again

2012 / 2017 / 2020 / 2021 / 2022

THE CHILD OF THE SACRED COW

Do you remember the day?
That dress I loved
Off white and roses
On the hill
The poet Skloot brought us to
The Pacific Ocean over there
And the sunlight in your yellow hair
And the kind of soft warm breeze
We would meet again in Venice later
Do you remember how we loved?

On that hill in Oregon

Do you remember when your whole sweet soul
Yearned for our boys to be?
How you watched all day for me
And I would come to you
And you took me in our bed
To the Moon and the stars beyond it

And the last one Nathaniel
The child of the sacred cow's sacrifice
What a wonderful woman you are
Wonderful and womanly

2012 / 2017 / 2020 / 2021 / 2022

DROWNED

The sharks circled
For no reason but to kill
Or die trying
To go back into the water
Was not a good idea

But I was marooned
The only way
To get back home to you
Was to swim for it

The raging waves broke
Marking time
In the time between
The lightning flashes and thunder claps
Twelve seconds to the mile away

Even then I understood
It might be a mirage
Yet I waited
And you slipped away
For nothing

And if those silver carnivores were real
What could they have done to me
That's worse than losing you?
There is no life in a body stripped of its soul

Like Hartley's gift to the poet Crane
Eight Bells
A million eyes stare up at me
Through indigo waters
The deep blue depths
Watched as I decide
To swim for my life

To find you my love
And on the way perhaps
Reclaim my sunken heart
Before it is forever drowned

2012 / 2017 / 2020 / 2022

A WALK AND AFTER

Below the cloud circus
The water raged
To a rhythm of its own
The wind made mad music

Dervish like the blown sand swirled
The dance a gritty minuet
The dog and I walked the winter beach
Alone
Snow covered to the waterline
Where the foam and sea-scum sculpted
An ever changing edge
Depending on the size of the break

The Scruffy dog chased the gulls
I thought of you

Sometime after
The steel gray clouds
Took on a backlit eggplant glow
The temperature plunged
The waves changed
Ten foot water mountains some of them

Then snow fell
And it fell hard
It became difficult to see
Where the water and the sand met
And the white glare hurt my semitic eyes

Made to see in the desert

I whistled for the dog
Fearing that with the gulls
And by then the wet salty spray
The crashing of the breaking waves
With all the bluster and the din of it
The dog would not hear me

But as always he returned
Proud of his comprehension
His ability to differentiate
Between my whistle
And the other noise

He was panting from the effort spent
Chasing the gulls
That I suspect he knew he'd never catch
In the cold and driving snow
That covered him

So old friend
Should we go home where she's waiting
Or should we hunker down
Beneath the boardwalk for a while?
The dog stared at the sea
At ease with the wildness
Then he turned
His floppy eared head towards me
As if I said something interesting

Perhaps it was the gulls he never caught
Taunting him
Maybe they were daring him to chase them again
To play some more
Like Human Beings who chase their lovers
Until they're caught
By the lover they chased

I became angry
But not at the weather or the gulls or the dog
I was angry with myself for getting stuck in it
Conflicted
Between my need to be with her
And my physical state that required rest

We made for the boardwalk
I mean my dog and I
Let us rest a bit and I will dream of her
And you can dream of catching gulls

Under the boardwalk now
My back against a concrete post
I faced the white
I felt afloat in it

Now the wind tore at us
And like the swirling snow
We spun around in vortexes
Weightless and afraid
Fighting to hold on
Anchored to that pillar

I held tight to the dog for dear life

But the dog was the first to fly away
Into the weather and the white and the noise
I soon gave up my hold

Trusting Fate
Fate
That from time's beginnings
Conspired
To bring my dog and me there then

I closed my eyes and fantasized
About how she would greet us
When we returned to her
(That is if we ever did)

The way she would fuss
Over that Scruffy dog
Drying him head to tail
Adoringly
Acting as if she was mad at me
I mean mad as Hell
For causing her to worry so

A moment later
We would be making love
Anywhere that was flat enough
Our bed
The kitchen table
The floor
Until the storm stopped
That at the time we hoped never would

And the dog would sleep
And dream of the shore birds
He would catch tomorrow.

2013 / 2017 / 2020 / 2021 / 2022

APOLOGY

Sudden rupture
A painful tear
The evanescent clouds parted
Magic was in the air

But still I suffered
A love laden longing
Soul sick
Incomplete
Until you

Neither the Sun
Nor Zindel's Marigold Moon
Not the ultra of the calmed sea
Far beyond the breaking waves
Nor the falling of the water-mountains
Blasting beach boundaries

Not the music the birds made
Nor the Lord's lavender skies
Nor the fine blue Kentucky grass
That begat you
And those notched eyes of yours
Full souled and gorgeous

Nothing prepared me
For your special splendor
Dazzled
You took my breath away

But time and separation are poison to love
And also age decays

The strange and glorious Truth ?
In all the years we spent together
And all the love we made
And with all the miles and time between us
I have never loved you more

But how could I then know
You knew not yourself?
You're deeper than the black abysmal
I could not find the bottom of you

Hotter than the whitest star
Brighter
More woman
More wonderful than I knew

And more I think than was known by you
For if you knew
You would have known
I was never worthy

Though now I am but half alive
I love you madly

I thought I should
I could possess you
But now I see I blocked your sun
I tried to keep the rain away
I stole the air around you
(You and the precious love we shared)
I made you blind
To shield you from the pain I saw
And deaf
For I monopolized the music

Now you're in the sun
Loving the nurturing rain
In the world you see the blessings
More than the pain
Self-sufficient
Life adept without me

I thought you would like to know
That now too late
I know it too
This poem is my apology
This sadness
The product of my sins

2013 / 2017 / 2020 / 2021 / 2022

IRONY

Vincent died of loneliness
An angel with a broken heart
A victim of his pain
His work stacked in Theo's house
For them there was no gain
Now wicked men pay mightily
For a piece of him

The only piece of Paradise
They will ever own
Purchased by money
Acquired in sin

He died in anonymity
Now universally known
Big enough for Vincent
The needle's eye too small
For the fat men with the money
Who hang Vincent
On their stuccoed
Cross beamed walls

Vincent's work was what it was
When few cared at all
Nothing changed but fashion
Perversity has been around
Long before the fall

An insult to his sacrifice
This scene he would abhor
Only Jesus in all history
Would ever hate it more

It's hard to take the irony
Life can be so mean

The greed is all encompassing
A hundred million for his sweat
Paid for by those who live for gold
Those who want to show the world
There's nothing they can't get

Give Vincent his materials
Perhaps a starry night
And he would be content
So destitute in other ways
Theo forced to pay his rent

Now Vincent is big business
The prices for his paintings astronomical
Funny when you think of it
Vincent died for painting love

An angel with a job to do
Vincent lived for something fine
He strove to make the world more beautiful
His work is of the Lord
Divine
Painting Heaven's holy hope and dreams
Singing hymns in color chords

2013 / 2017 / 2020 / 2021 / 2022

BETTER DAYS

The north wind blows the sand around
The sea to molten lead
The waves make their symphonies

How far did these water mountains roll
Before breaking on this little island
I call home ?

I'm grateful for the music of the sea
Its salty spray
And the color of the briny light
The setting sun
Moves from rose to purple plum and gray
I take for a sign of better days

It's more than fifty years
Since I last stood
With my father here
At the end of the world
That place where the swirling sand meets the sea

He said
Long after he and I were gone
This scene in different moods would play
And would until the Sun turned black
He reckoned 'bout six billion years

And then the Earth
With nothing to keep it in its orbit
Would spin off to another place
In the universe

Now I see he must have known
His time here was very near its end
He was preparing my solace
In the vastness
And my joy in the immensities
For a man's life
Even his
Is a puny thing and small

More than anything
He wished for me love
He said
In the end it's only love
A soul can hang onto

The thing to do is to play the role assigned me
He said he would visit me
From time to time
At least his spirit would
And he told me not to worry
There's precious little we can control
If anything at all

Man's future is
And will always be
A mystery to him
And all his plannings and contingencies
A waste of fucking time

When I leave this place
I want to live with you again
To take the children to that beach
My soul's foundation
To tell them what my father said
Those many years ago

To sit and watch the water
To wonder at it all
To hear the sea's ever changing symphonies
To see the move from night to day
To cause the color change
Presenting Actuality

Each day to catch a glimpse of Heaven
If we look hard enough

Do you remember when I first brought you there ?
We stayed at Bruce's mother's place
You told me secrets of your past
Afraid that I would leave you
You could not believe my love was actual
Or you were afraid to

Maybe
The love in which you could not believe
Was your own
For I have loved you from the moment we met
And for what it's worth to you
If anything at all
I always will

You caused a scene
At the Kosher Deli
With your Irish green benotched eyes
Your yellow hair
A stranger in a strange land
If ever there has been one

And the yentas yented
And we laughed until we cried
Like we often did back then
When the world was young
And there was only you and I

2013 / 2017 / 2020 / 2021 / 2022

THE DEVIL'S DANCE

I sing the American Requiem
A discordant carnival
A song of decadence
Where law is defined
By soulless sinners
Fat and rich
They kill old dreams
And those who dare to dream them

America is dying
A dirge played in a minor key
So near the end
Of this false reality

Orpheus in the underworld
Faust in his own damnation
There is a mental illness here
Prognosis for this nation

Poor

Where Bezos is Jesus Christ the Lord
Gates the Prophet John
Buffet the apostle Peter
The rock the church is built upon
Where Cheney at the age of seventy
Cut the line to take a young man's heart
To replace his damaged one
Few would believe he ever owned

Greed robs the rich man's soul
As if their money is not enough
Their lust for more pure gluttony
Their power grab
Has made slaves of us
We the people are no longer free

But enough of this except to say
The Devil's dancing
To Satan's music
On the corpse of The U. S. A.

2013 / 2017 / 2020 / 2021 / 2022

ODYSSEY

The lamentation music
Made mad opera sounds
Howling witches
The madder moon
Here we sing of death and longing
An unattractive song
Yet popular with metaphysicians
And they are rarely wrong

Setting sail
I am dreaming
'Round the world!
The mastheads cry
But there will be
No circumnavigation
The oceans gone bone dry

Still
The spirit waters roll and rock me
Odysseus of the bedroom
Sails these seas from home
Navigating by line and log
For my compass has been long broken

The drunken sailors dance
The moonlight madness
Speaking of mutiny
'Tis not the captain they'll be overthrowing
Not Gods
Not kings
Not me

It was Satan's voice spoke revolution
Too much owned by those of means
No truth now in the prophet's words
No honor in the poet king

We are left to make this journey
Beneath starless skies
We sail before the wind
But only the dead are reckoning
Drifting on this sea of ash and bone

Whirlwinds whip Hell's fires
They burn but shed no light
The deluge floats Dante's barque
In this sea of wordless woe

Their mutiny too little
Too fucking late

No air to let the spirit breathe
Heaven's boundaries rent
And the fools expect redemption
But it will not be sent
The raging waves
Tell fairy tales

Silent storms
Violate the sky
Black lightning
Dooms the Devil's demons
Upon their Hellish thrones

I swim the seas of oblivion
Satan's minions tear at me
From Heaven's holy light I fell
And I am still falling

Like a beacon in the heart of darkness
Your eyes in place of stars
You are my guide
My direction home
My redemption
And my resurrection

I will return to you
To beg your love
Once more
To offer up my heart to you
My soul's forever wife

2013 / 2017 / 2020 / 2021 / 2022

A PAIR OF SINS

Your notched eyes on any other face
Would be a pair of gorgeous sins
But on your face they are an angel's
Mountain movers
They speak words
Which sound like prayer
When you cry
The earth is nourished by your tears

I think of you
And I forget this cage
In which I live
And the fucking freaks
Who tell me what to do

I tell them not to judge me
To turn their moral compass to themselves
That they dare not try to take my soul
Until they own their own

But even then
My soul is all I am
I'll not surrender it
Without a fight

Unless you
My love
Want it with the rest of me
Yours forever
Anyway

2013 / 2017 / 2020 / 2021 / 2022

MEMORIAL

The surf was up that Friday
The big boys roaring
Crests of foam
The northeast wind propped them up
The waves I mean
Some of them eight feet
The sky portended rain
My home
My beach
Paradise

The tide washed up
An old man's junk
Note filled bottles
Barrel staves
Black Beard's own treasure map
A gold doubloon
The remnants of a galleon
Ahab's blood-tempered harpoon
A Horseshoe crab in its carapace

The gull earns his morning meal
He circles then dives deep for it
Then holds off the skulking birds
Waiting
To pick their spots
To take his catch away
To earn their food the easy way

Pushy pushy pushy
Best to let the mad dogs lay
The mean sons-a-bitches that they are

Bobby
Beachcomber
Wakes at noon
To miss another day of work
He pops a can of Bud first thing
Lights the day's first cigarette
Watching the tide roll in

He has already paid a lifetime's worth of dues
Sitting there with his beer
Thinking of the beaches
He left behind in 'Nam

Crazy Louie lived to surf
He moved to Hawaii
For the weather and the waves

He died
Around the time Bobby did
Each far too young a man

But they lived more in their short lives
Than many much older men
Louie road the curl
Hanging ten
On the big Waikikian waves
Bobby kept beach combing
To the end

We had so many plans together
For living our old age
But as they so often do
Life and death got in the way

Now Bobby combs
Heaven's spotless beaches
Watching
Louie ride the perfect waves
And I live behind these walls
In this cage
Alone but for these ghosts
That sometimes keep me company

I think I hear your voice at times
I'm happy for a while
I find light and hope
In your conversation
Who cares if it is real?

2013 / 2017 / 2020 / 2021 / 2022

LIKE JOJO LAST MONDAY (THROUGH MELVILLE'S EYES)

When one prefers their dreams
To the life they live
Like I do
When one longs for yesterday
Instead of looking towards tomorrow
When the only wonder a new day brings
Is to wonder how you will get through it
When it hurts to think of going on with life
When one becomes too old or sick
To hunt the great leviathan
It is natural then
And noble
And even wise
To wish for death
The time when one's soul set free
Like JoJo's was
Last Monday

Let us mourn for ourselves at her loss
But celebrate her freedom
For us her loss is the pain
She will no longer have to bear

And we will weep
And feel a fathomless sorrow
In our loneliness
But we should know
And keep in mind
That Jo will never hurt again

Shooting stars burn out
Before the duller ones in Heaven
And birds that fly in the mountain hollows
Soar higher than those that fly over the plains
Goodbye my cousin
Adios my friend
There is so much in life and death
We will never comprehend

2013 / 2017 / 2020 / 2021 / 2022

BLACK STOCKINGS

It's bliss to watch the one you love sleeping
Smiling in a peaceful dream
Somehow knowing you're awake
Protecting her

Loving you

The point at which
As individuals
You cease to exist
For a time
Obliterate
Where one ends
And the other begins

A half clad woman
A black bustier
Beautiful and lusting
Black stockings

Removed in haste to please you
Undergarments
Strewn around the room
Trusting you

A boundless faith
All romance a discovered bliss
You become her and she you
Betrayal here a suicide

But love's joys
Too soon take flight with laughter
To cease but for the memories
Memories of happy times
That to remember hurts

Thinking back to what once was
You would think we'd find some joy in reminiscing
While we love
Let's die in it

Die together hand in hand
To find ourselves in Paradise
Where the joy of love
Is part of us forever

You are my love
A shooting star
You are my angel
Heaven sent and radiant
I hear the sound of your holy wings
As you sit beside me
I am entranced
By your benotched eyes
Awful for their great beauty
And for their power over me

There is magic in your breathing
My heart and soul moves towards yours
You fly I follow
The Universe is you and I

Touch me with your eager hands
Let your yellow hair fall on me
Kiss my loving eyes
The air champagne around you
You quicken me with longing

You defy all laws of aging
Exempt from decay
But if ever outward loveliness
Departs from you
Your inner beauty will replace
The departing loveliness
Beauty of a different kind
Higher and more holy

O that you could see my heart
You would know all I've tried
To express to you in words

2013 / 2017 / 2020 / 2021 / 2022

LOST

The cloudy sky cast blue light
That filled the massive dome
The place Saint Peter sleeps
Bernini's Baldacchino
A football field away

Behind me to the right
A niche
A pieta made by God
With the help of the young Michaelangelo

Then the light changed to gold
A mystic luminosity
And the motes of holy dust danced
To the music of some sacred breeze
In this church where the inside can be mistaken
For the outside in its scale
And the streaming light half-shadowed
Like the darkness of multitudinous moons

And I heard blessed Mary
Cry for all the children
As she held own son crucified
This sculpture is a miracle

I held onto you
As not to fly away
Like forever in my dreams
I allowed myself to soar
Knowing
I could always count on us

But I should have let you know
What it was I was attempting
I should not have assumed
That you would understand

Holding you as if I held the Universe
Until you let me go
My soul is sadly shaken
My broken heart roars
Torments of doubt and shame

Beyond the limits of belief
And tolerance and pain

Lost
I'm soul searching for the holy places
My heart tells me
Are still there to find
Before the darkness
And the ungodly cold

Useless meanderings
So much wasted time

There is mercy in ignorance
Godliness can be a melancholy thing

I hold no hate or malice now
Too old to spend that kind of energy
I'll away with negativity
As much as it's in my power to
At least in my own life
For who am I to wish
Malevolence
On any other Man?

It becomes so clear
When the end is near
Ironically

Now that I've discovered how
I lack the strength to fly

2013 / 2017 / 2020 / 2021 / 2022

LOVE POEM

Though it makes us vulnerable
We must never cease to trust
It is simply the price
For the gift
That comes with being chosen
And the tears we cry the cost of loving
Of coming close to joy

You are my lover
My forever wife
You are my sun and moon
My sea and sky
My teacher
My best friend
My muse
My most marvelous dream
You are my life my all my everything

So you must know how the silence stabs
The day you left you took the color with you
The world has turned the darkest blue
Very close to black

Some lovers talk silently
Some with damaged voices
That come with telling lies
But you speak from your soul
And wordlessly
Fluent
In love's language
Through your notched eyes

Always seeking can make men moody
Always angling for experience
Like fighting for the Truth

But I've never had to look too far for beauty
With you by my side
And I've never had to search the heavens for an angel
All I had to do was reach for you instead

2013 / 2017 / 2020 / 2021 / 2022

SUMMER MUSIC

The thick fog drifted through our open door
Buoy bells rang the blues
As the fishing boats returned
From the Outer Banks
Bursting
Horns singing for safety's sake
And harmony
To celebrate the catch

And the gulls sang bird operas
Arias in the key of scream
And the wind howled
From the night's big blow

Summer music

It was early still
You were sleeping
In our bedroom down the hall
Over the outdoor shower
Where we made love
When we couldn't wait to get inside
Any place was perfect
When you were in the mood

And I stayed close
Just in case you needed me
In the bushes near that museum
The rest stop along the road
The way you answered Kristina O
On the shores of Winnipesaukee
The many venues for our loving
The best times of my life

What a ride we had my darling
What a woman you are my love

I sat outside for a while
In that salt sodden mist
To wait on the Sun

You must have rolled over then
Found I was not next to you
You called for me

We walked the beach towards the eastern end
You and me and Benny in your belly
And that scruffy dog
And the sun shone
On the wave crests whitening
Before they broke
As they must
Shattered
Unnumbered shards of foam

There is a certain smell on the beach
That always brings me home
And there is the certain smell of you
I taste you still
And sup on the hope I have

A Limbodian now
A citizen
Of the suburbs of Hell

And the mad dogs of glory howl
Their cheap discordancies
Unmolested even idolized
And Truth sits in silent places
Being made and found
By the few
Who seek it still
Only for itself

2013 / 2017 / 2020 / 2021 / 2022

THE LUNATIC'S RODEO

Mazeppa like
We ride the painted pony of Fate
The world goes 'round
A carousel that only stops
When Death intervenes

But while it turns
We never cease
Reaching for the golden ring
Without the curiosity
To try to learn
Why it is we almost always fail

There is no folly of any beast on Earth
That is not outdone
By the madness of Man

Naked ride the wild ones
In the lunatics' rodeo
White rabbits are the sages now
And the blasphemous media kings

The most fantastic works of man
Have not yet been written
And perhaps will never be

O you money-men
Killers of the human soul
Beware of Judgment Day
For all the money in the world
Can not keep you
Out of Hell

Useless in Heaven
It's love that's the coin of that realm
And the needle's eye is very small
Indeed

But God
Will never turn away
From those
Who earnestly seek Him

2013 / 2017 / 2020 / 2021 / 2022

HAMMER

Tragedy can be rife with beauty
Brings a bit of joy to my isolation
For the memories it conjures up
But a warning too
Frightened souls and death need wings to fly
And genius to find the word again
And always God's sweet intervention

There's a kind of dignity in death
Safe harbor
For a bruised and battered soul

Wild cyclonic churning wind
The falling up
Back to the light
From whence we first fell

Re-enfold me in your arms and legs
Our bodies one eternally

No coward's heart
My soul's my strength
But I'm ignorant
And often blind

Yet I can see what may be
When I look
I find no future
Without a you and me

Gabriel
Blow your gorgeous golden horn
To the brand new moon
Let us watch the saved souls
Soar
And love
And hope

Cling hard in the tempest winds
Fear not the wild waters
Respect them

Let us live in faith
For we are blessed
Never to know fear again
But it's the sound of woe
The wailing of the multitudes
That so upsets my soul
And even if I was disposed to laughter
Who can laugh with all the pain?

We should know better than to celebrate
Our rare moments of good fortune
While somewhere in the world
The children suffer so
I have seen their parents in despair
While they watched their children starve to death

So hold close the ones you love
Thank your God of choice
But remember when the good times come again
(And they will)
No one is immune
To Fate's heavy hammer

2013 / 2017 / 2020 / 2021 / 2022

AHAB'S BOAT

Like algae in The White Whale's wake
Phosphorescent
Light shines on the sea of Truth
Makes it possible to see

Time and close attention
Reveal true meaning
For those of us who need to know
Those brave enough
To search for it
Sometimes stove
Like Ahab's boat

All the wildest winds of Hell
Conspire to restrain
The spirit meant to soar
Promote the Devil's dirty work
To hide Truth in the great lie
It would be better for the spirit killed
Searching for experience
Than to spend eternal life with a stunted soul

Give me the strength to strive
Let my reach exceed my grasp
Like the great ones with exquisite courage
Who strove after Truth before
Knowing in advance that they would fail

Like the brave souls now drowned
Who gave their life to chase The White Whale
A pursuit that will never end
So long as there is human life on Earth

Youth is indeed wasted
On the young enough to own the moment
And the courage or the ignorance
To seek unafraid
Though with their inexperience
They know not what to search for
Like Ishmael who learned too late
And The Polish Rider
Forever young and arrogant

2013 / 2017 / 2020 / 2021 / 2022

TRIO

The Earth is a soggy bog of black blood
Soaked through with it
The crust?
Our father's bones
And of those of whom money-men call righteous
Men who justify their murdering
In whatever they believe that they believe
Or carrying out the orders
Of tired old malevolent men
Who tell them whom and when and where and how to kill
But very rarely why
They wield the power
We ourselves bestowed on them

We will hold them responsible
For the death of the innocents
For ignoring God's commandment
Thou shalt not kill
Damn them to Hell!

And we hold fast
To all of our irrelevant defiances
That belong in the sixties
For which we risk nothing now
No one fucking cares

I care not for the time I die
In other words when

Or what it is that finally kills me
In other words how

I do not wish to know the name of my killer
If murdered I am
In other words who

But I care a lot
For what my life and death might mean
In other words why
What good is life if you cannot choose
What you want to live and die for?

Like Jesus did
Like Martin and Malcolm too
Like so many other nameless martyred saints

2013 / 2017 / 2020 / 2021 / 2022

UNSETTLED TIME

St. Elmo's fires flash false witness
Star events roil the darkened sky
A glimpse of evil and lightning strikes

Those with souls calm enough
Move toward the gathering place
On the fields of Armageddon

Now malefactors named the righteous ones
Mock those they do not slay
Bandits steal their lover's hearts
Take their innocence away
Lying lips and vast deceptions
Pride fueled doers
Hard-hearted men
The world is mad and badly used
The holy rain is fast approaching
Get ready for the deluge
Get ready for the end of days

Sycophantic devil dancers
Take joy in their malevolence
Making soundless noise
And these scoundrels sell resurrection
Like fish
So much the pound

Offered wisdom sageless clowns
Treacherous fools
And Godless phantoms
Gathered on the hallowed ground
Defended by youth slingshotted
Like once the poet warrior king
Looking for redemption
Unlikely to be found

Pranksters and punks with nothing to lose
Can also read the signs
Too late to get to righteousness
They frolic in their shame
Their souls condemned

There is a kind of Hell born freedom
Anything goes makes men mad
And dangerous
A wild unsettled time
God knows

The plagued Earth reeks pestilence
Like The Reapers rancid breath
Foretellers of the end of days
Around us only death

Let me help the sainted stay
And fight
Martyrs for the Holy Word
I've lived enough
To end my life
By standing up for righteousness

2013 / 2014 / 2017 / 2020 / 2021 / 2022

VAPORS AND STARRY BEASTS

Add my grief
To the whole of the world's woe
The kind of pain by which
You and I were always moved

This is the way
The world has always rolled
The haves and the have nots

A bruised heart
A roiled soul
Two more fucking fools

I live alone in a sideless house
And hang
The paintings I made for you
On walls of air

Sanctimonious scoundrels
Have torn us apart
But they know not your heart
Nor my own

Some things like love
Will never be denied
Woe to the fool
Who would deny them

Sometimes when the icy winds
Drive away vague vapors
The sky fills with starry beasts
On a good night
A zoo's worth
While here on Earth
The moon shines on the circus

2013 / 2017 / 2020 / 2021 / 2022

AMBIGUITIES

The world is full of neglected sons
And those who think they are
Who wish their fathers dead
Now and then like Smerdyakov
They even make it happen

And when their fathers finally pass away
These abandoned boys of all ages know not
If they should dance for joy
Or mourn
Or cry
Or pray

We love them but we hate them too
The best of them at that
It may well be
The better the father is at fathering
The more he is despised

Whatever else we might conclude
We cannot hate ourselves for hating them
Often for no apparent reason

Because they begat us ?

We hold them responsible
For the fucked up lives we live
And it's the more a convolution
When we become fathers of sons too
Especially while remaining sons
To better men

Fathers are like kings
To their parricidal sons
They are all - powerful
And if that is not enough
To wish them dead
Our sainted mothers are their lovers

We their sons
Wait for our ascension
But when our fathers die
It's like the death of a God

Ahab and Starbuck were fathers too
Did Jesus feel that way about both of his ?

Life is the swing and flow of constant change
We shed our skins many times before our end
Eight billion fucking snakes
And our souls evolve each time we do
So many metamorphoses

Born many times to the same life
Each time around in many ways
Almost unrecognizable
So we clutch to our first identities
Try to disown our changes
Like the butterfly that acts like the worm

Most men are afraid to learn
We lack the courage to dare
Captive to our consciousness
Chained to responsibility
No wonder man is mad

Some victims know they sometimes own
A small share of the blame
We suffer to better understand our dreams
Searching for the place we went astray

All we know for sure is
We have endured so far
Endured the agony
Of that enduring
If nothing else a miracle
A testament to fortitude

We play life like the blues

In the music of our pain
There is the light of Man's flamed faith
And every now and then
We triumph over helplessness
And yes Man is Man
But Man is also marvelous
Damned and holy and ambiguous

2013 / 2017 / 2020 / 2021 / 2022

DEATH THE DANCER

In the briefest moment
That flash of the time of our full flowering
When we have gone as high as we can go
When our senses are strong enough
To recognize the Truth
At the cresting of the wave
We must remind ourselves
Time is short
Between birth and death
Should you live to be a hundred years

All the while
The Reaper waits
To carry us away
Death the dancer needs a partner
For the final pas de dieux

You taught me to live
But who is there
To teach me how to die?

The silence crescendos
An inverted wall of silent sound
Like those days of quiet thunder
And dry rain
When black showed white
And up was down
And I was truly happy

But fantasies and dreams
Are for the young

And we have been known
To invent our own promises
I've lived too many moons
I've suffered too much fucking pain
To waste my precious time
Wishing
I'd live long enough to understand

Over time my body grew
In more or less the way prescribed
Well nourished
The boy became a man
But the growth of my soul was less linear

But it's just as likely
And maybe more
The Human Soul is fully formed at birth
Living is the cause
Of the soul's great grief
And diminishment

I am ravaged by denial and sin
I've paid the price to find my better promise

It's easier to believe in God
Than put one's hope in the goodness of Man
Yet with all our sins
We may still shine
Like the good
Who struggle for the Ideal

And though they may fall short in life
It is freedom won in the pursuit
Their souls are free to fly away
Unfettered by regret
For the game of life too often lost
In what we believe to be it's winning

All the while
The Reaper waits
To carry us away
Death the dancer needs a partner
For the final pas de dieux

2014 / 2017 / 2020 / 2021 / 2022

A MILLION WAYS

The stars like diamonds
Fire forged
The fire vortex
Paint Van Gogh pictures in the sky
And the waves spin white
Phosphorescent spray
When the shore break reclaims the sea-scum
From the ebb

Horizoned boat lights shine like fallen ones
And I pray
O Lord with your holy tears
Wash my sins away
And drown the Hell's hot fire
That burns within me

Suddenly the sky was filled
With light and many angels
Gabriel on his golden horn
Sounded a lot like Miles
And Michael on the Devil's neck
Sweet Jesus in his fire chariot
Came to save
Reward the meek
And to keep His other promises

And I wept for all the beauty
This kind of glory never meant
For sinners' eyes like mine to see
But this was not the first time
I was blessed like this

The hotel garden
In east Africa
Where we first kissed
And all the times after
We made love
And all the plans we made
In our life together
And every single day
I woke up beside you

The beach has always been for me
A place for dreams and visions
When I was young
I could swear that I could fly

The past plays memory games

But if I ever stopped remembering
I'd be left with only pain
I don't know if I could stand it
Or if I'd want to live that way

The Human Heart is hard to read
Many fathoms deep
Like glass in its fragility
A million ways to bleed

An artist's soul is an open wound
And there's nothing for the pain but work
The agony
Fuel for his fire

Talent is but a tenth part
Of that which makes an artist great
The rest is the artist's sweat
And will
Belief and desire

2014 / 2017 / 2020 / 2021 / 2022

NEPTUNIA

There
At the end of the landed world
Where the sand meets the roaring sea
And the scale is made by seabirds
Or the spar
Of some horizoned ship

There
Is the real and constant power
Heartless
Always beautiful
And also very dangerous

For the ocean is a gorgeous lady
Call her Neptunia
Love her
But beware of her as well

Then there is the vastness
That makes us understand
The pointlessness of fear
The puniness of man
And the salted light so well remembered
And walking in my father's footprints
In the wet sand

These memories behind these walls
Makes me yearn for freedom more
And all my lost loves
That place that was my home
And the sky above
The immensities

Black clouds and raging waters
Lighting zaps and thunder claps
The sand turned to pellets by the gales
And dervishes
Horizontal rain
And the breaking waves
Overstepping

The highest of the highest tides
Crash against the dunes
Meant to stop the ocean waters
From mixing with the waters of the bay

And a few
Like Crazy Louie
Ride
The white crested water mountains
Before they break
Water shards
As many as the stars

The whining of the wires
On the shore road
Where berefuged gulls sit watching
Nature's show

And you and I are making love
While outside
All Hell is breaking loose
Knowing if the flood came
We would be carried off together

2014 / 2017 / 2020 / 2021 / 2022

CONTRADICTIONS

Civilized
Calm
In the middle of pandemonium
The amalgamation of evil and good
Lovers
Of enlightenment and poetry

Yet it doesn't take a lot for us to kill
When we are in the mood
We are good and beautiful
Possessed by high ideals
As long as they are easy to fulfill

Sometimes Angelic
But mostly
We are greedy
And for money insatiable
Yet when we have it
We piss it away

Clusters of contradictions
We are composed of ambiguity
Thoughtless and depraved
Yet noble too
With our lofty ideals

Impudent
Impetuous
But also high-minded
And magnanimous
We are generous with the money we steal

Church goers on Sundays
Criminals the rest of the week
Full of shit
Yet often as honest as ole Abe
Liars
Searching for the Truth

We stand at the abyss
Wretched and dissatisfied
Incomplete
But big enough
To yearn for Heaven
And strong enough to endure

Haters of other persons
We love all of humanity
A sense of degradation
Required
For our well being
Like our honor is

We are all sane
We are all crazy
The inmates are once again
Running the asylum
And everything is OK

We need to work
But never tire
Serve humanity silently
With great humility

Never lose heart

Abandoned by everyone
Driven out by force
Banished and alone
The struggle is to keep faith

We water the Earth with our tears
And trust the Earth to bring salvation
We will be redeemed

Stand strong in your beliefs
Though in this world
You are the only person
Who believes them
Truth is no democracy
The majority rarely rules
Rejoice in the righteous ones

Be wary of the world
Yet never despise it
For there
But for the grace of God
Goes everyone

Do not fear or be alarmed
At your ecstasy
For it is a gift

We stand
Between eternal life
And this existence
We must pray
For those
Overcome by woe

One of the hardest things
A man can do
Is to accept another's love
But when we do
We are in fact
Loving the other person back
Requiting all the love we get
In equal or greater measure

When we give we receive

The body and the soul are one
One grows in ways programed genetically
Flesh and bone
Sinew and blood

Formed to exist
To hide and seek
Reinventing ourselves with hope
Amidst all the contradiction
And ambiguity

We make our plans
Captivated
By our petty mysteries
We dream our dreams
Then work like Hell
To make them manifest

But the world seems too big for us
The dreams get out of hand
And we are crushed

Ravaged by actuality
Drained of all our energy
Damaged beyond repair

Fucked up beyond all recognition
Broken to pieces
On the wall of Truth
Crucified

We ask nothing for ourselves
Save for good health
A little bit of happiness
And to remember

We fought hard
We never retreated
Or surrendered
But we were overwhelmed
We had our asses kicked
We were destroyed

Still sometimes our old eyes flash

We sit and wait
And it is awful
All a man can do
Is his best
As he sees his best to be
And know
There are no guarantees

There is a healing wonder in remembering
To look for satisfaction
From our life's work
And look forward to the moment of our freedom
When our souls will be released

Death is liberation

2014 / 2017 / 2020 / 2022

CLOWNS

Your silences
Are by far the louder
Of the whisperings
And the raging waves
Louder than the howling tempest winds
The stormy booming breaking seas
Your silent screams are killing me

Tormented by society
I have greatly aged
Countless tears
Have damned my troubled eyes
I am sinking
Slowly dying
Suffering so

But worst of all
Is the pain of losing you

More people die of heartbreak
Than all known disease
And I died a little more today

I bleed
But there is no blood to see
And the strengths
Once proudly possessed by me
Ebb like tides away
And the Hell-fires burn
And the wicked woe

But the promise remains
All sins will be forgiven
Purified in the holy water
And by the holy light
On Judgment Day

The prophets have been discredited
By those who pull the strings
Though the prophets see with crystal clarity
They're ridiculed for their sanity
While the money-men
Sell their lies as true

When facts point to their conspiracies
They label them lunatic imaginings
The prophets are God's chosen ones
But the money- men and their sycophants
Turn them into clowns

And jails are actually filled with the innocent
Some of whom have been a long time down
Some sit on Death-Row
Waiting for their state sponsored deaths
For crimes that weren't theirs

Privacy has been pirated
By the so called patriots
When they tell you something is
You can bet that it is not
Like when they tell you
The thirteenth
Is the fourteenth floor
When they say one plus one
Is always two

No matter what the risk
Never stop questioning
Shout freedom from the darkest places
Like here where I am shouting from
Blow up that joyous horn

For Mickey Mouse is finally dead
Goose stepping
With his father Walt
In Disneyland
Another name for Hell

We are free to live our dreams
On the wings of our own imaginings
That cartoon rodent rat-fuck fascist vermin
Dead at last
Motherfucking Mickey Mouse
Taken out
By those who guard the light

2014 / 2017 / 2020 / 2021 / 2022

MOON HOWLING

It is hard enough to be in here
Without the way I deal with it
The only person here to talk with
Is myself
But I no longer like the company

One day I was with the ones I love
And I was free
The next one solo
Dancing
To the music of woe
Locked up in here
In misery
In the hottest heat of Hell

I'm so damned sick of the inner voices
I cannot help but hear
Driven to distraction
I know not how to make them stop
Other than the obvious
But I'm not built that way
And suicide
An awful song of sorrow anyway

Heavy souled and broken hearted
Stuck between this so called life
And sweet annihilation

I'm a sailor on a sea of love
A soul astronaut
A moon howler
Howling at the moon
Tough enough to howl again
At that orange orb
That fills the space between the iron bars
Makes your spirit known once more
For there you are listening
For some sign of life

And the same moon
That lights my cell tonight
Lights your life with holy light
And you will know
It is I moon howling
Who else behaves that way?

We are creatures of the middle ground
Stuck between the radiance
And the darkness of the grave

I'm confused by all the choices
Rarely sure of anything
But for death
Clutching at belief
Based on love not fear

Better to laugh out loud
At all the human paradox
That in the end
Doesn't mean a fucking thing
Less important to the workings of the Universe
Than the smallest grain of sand
To a beach

If I wasn't so damned tired
I'd run another lap around this life
But only if I knew for sure
That you would be a part of it
I'd like another chance
To get it right
To learn from my mistakes
To rejoice that I've lived long enough
To make them

An atmospheric glitch turned the stars green
Like your notched eyes
My heart is hot for you tonight
The moon is passion filled

2014 / 2017 / 2020 / 2021 / 2022

THE COURAGE IT TAKES

Lead white and rust
Some kind of acid yellow near to green
Turner paints Petworth's light
Inside the drawing room

Vincent loved it so
He literally ate it
The lead white paint I mean
And I would gladly eat it too
If I could paint like Vincent did
After I ate it
If I could see what Turner saw

Anyway
They don't make lead white paint any more

Turner was the greater man
For living on
Taking life on the chin
Lonely like Vincent was
But less in need of human company
And stronger
All alone
No support of kin

Turner was a working man
Vincent more an angel
But because he died the way he did
We will never know
How much greater than he was
Vincent might have been

2014 / 2017 / 2020 / 2021

HIGH STAKES AND HURRICANES

The fat cats want it all
And now they almost have it
Small payments to the middle class
Working jobs we mostly hate

And on our sweat the fat cats earn
Fifty times and more than their salaries
One thousand times more than ours

We all know about man's well laid plans
And how they're laid to waste
Too much talking
Destroys them in the end

Now faith will be required
To intervene for Truth again

The problem not so much
In their games fairly won
But that they play by their own rules
And they cheat the games
They've already fixed to win

The stakes as high as can be
In the murder and the mayhem
In all the fucking misery

Those who make their money making war
Very rarely send their own kids
To fight them
And when the killing stops
They are paid anew
For building back
That which they were paid
The first time to destroy

But this is all beside the point of living
To love and to create
What does the pursuit of more money
Have to do with revelation?
Why do we continue to play by their rules ?

Rules they have put in place
To keep the money with the very few

How does one sift through the shit
To get at Truth ?
So I scream into the hurricane
Knowing I cannot be heard
Against the wind

2014 / 2017 / 2020 / 2021 / 2022

WILD RICE AND CORNISH HENS

The music in Mozart's head
Melville's dreams
The colors on Vincent's color board
The words to an Ira Gershwin song
Brother George's rhapsodic taxi horn
They took joy in giving
But the greedy world wanted more
Than even they could give

Let me dry your eyes with my kisses
Take my hand
When Death comes for me
I'm already old
All you need to do is let me go

But never let us say goodbye
One last I love you
Will nicely do
Until the time
You too crossover

On the other side
I'll wait for you
Once joined two souls
Are forever tied
And no power known
But for God's alone
Can untie them

If you want to be with me
I'll wait a trillion trillion years
And many trillion more if I must
In speaking of death
One learns to talk in terms of eternity

When I come home
Let's take a house
On the rocky Irish coast
Near Donegal
Eat wild rice and Cornish Hens
Drink the local brew

Then venture up to Sligo
See Ben-Bulben from the poet's grave

I'll carve a shillelagh
Paint it green
To match your notched eyes
Make a painting
A picture of you
Naked in our single bed
In the morning
While you're still asleep

Later
Drink our fill of Irish Whiskey
Watch the movement of the blackened clouds
In the gray Donegalian sky
As they color the ocean
To the dark gray-green
Below the cliffs
Where our cottage sits

Then make love by the peat fire

Maybe make the trip to Dublin Town
Walk where Bloom and Dedalus did
Visit the college of the Trinity
Where the Dowden brothers
Taught the Bard

But in the end
I care not much
Where I am
So long as you are there

2014 / 2017 / 2020 / 2021 / 2022

NO MORE TALK

The storm blew up from the south
The water
Furious
Broke and groaned and foamed
The head on a salty beer

And the wicked winds howled
And the sky hung low and dirty
Like the smoke stained ceiling
In the Ice Man's bar

There was no sun or moon
Or stars
No night and day
Where Hickey drank
And had his say
Buying rounds for his boys

It was all I could do to stand and face
That fearsome savage sea
But better here confronting it
Than battened down in our house
Made anyway of straw

I was worried sick

I had no way to get to you
Suddenly the wind stopped
Soon after the rain
And the Sun
A holy rose
Broke through the clouds

Like light through a church window

But it was scary still
For I knew it wasn't over yet
The worst was yet to come

Then it occurred to me
There is as much or more
In the head of a man
Than all concealed
Beneath the sea

But the ocean has no ax to grind
Subject only to the will of God
And the Human Soul is many fathoms deep
Explore it
If you have the courage to

Sometimes even the sea is silent
But man is never mute
Better to stop talking
Better to stop making noise
Polluting the Universe
Driving the Martians mad

Look around
For in nature there are still
Signs of Truth to be found

Satan's minions sate themselves on envy's bread
Filled with hate and greed
Putting money before everything
Then they leave it to their evil seed
When they disappear

Like everyone naked
They come into the world
Interred in their most expensive suits
Their pockets stuffed with gold
Hey you never know
If to get through Heaven's gates
Requires
The payment of a toll

Laid out in their worm proof bronze boxes
More luxurious to their perverted minds
Than a simple box of wood
These motherfuckers see the bronze
As dying first class

All of this is worthless where they're going
In time the worms will get to them too
And their souls
(Such as they are)
Will burn and melt in Hell's hot fires
Eternal guests in Satan's home

2014 / 2017 / 2020 / 2021 / 2022

WHALE HUNTER

In the dead of night
In the desert of my all alone
In the whirlwind that dropped me here
Like Dorothy in Oz

I am full with wonder and why and woe
In the end I'm nothing but confused
Ready to stop the questioning
To accrue it to some fearsome will
But not my own or my earthly father's
Nor his
Nor his

It comes down to God I guess
To have his way with us

But the night gives no rest
The voices and the words
Which never come

We are left to and we must
Make rhyme and reason of the dread
Or find a cliff near the ocean
Off which
To leap into the sea

I will go whale hunting
Like Ahab chased the white Leviathan
To look for Truth
Or peace
But knowing better
Than to hope to capture
Either one of them

2014 / 2017 / 2020 / 2021 / 2022

ECCE HOMO

The landscape sat black silhouetted
The orange yellow streak weighed indigo
Levitating over all of it
The fields below just harvested
The morning after
A holy time of year
Magenta bled the sky
Now black and red and gray
Cobalt blue and lavender
Levin and his scythe

A picture
I painted of a memory

For the millionth time or more
I said out loud I love you
My heart is broken

Three years ago Christmas Eve
The papers from your lawyer came
Divorcing me
But paper means nothing to the Human Heart
And will never mean a thing to me
But as something on which to make my art
Or with which to wipe my ass

The winds of time cry work
If what one does is who they are
Then when one is gone
It's what he did
That makes a man who he was

Very soon I'll be no more
Life is but a one time thing
(In this form at least)

Gird for battle
Make sure you have your say
So when the darkness comes
Completely spent
There will be no need to rage

Ecce homo
I am Man
Here I am for all it's worth
Ashes to ashes
Earth to Earth

Now I pray for sleep

When I'm released
I'll walk up out of here
I'll find my way home to you
To offer up my love anew

I'm older now
But have not aged
My heart is badly bruised is all
Instead of the red it was
A funky shade of black and blue
But stronger than it was
Before the fall

I admit that I have changed
Less ambitious as to worldly things
And more for some kind of God belief
An artist
A seeker of Truth

A fucking fool
On fire for you

I don't speak much these days
But learned to communicate
In other ways
I do OK with pen and paint
Mostly I discover how I really feel

I'm witness now to many things
I've seen Man"s brutality
Their need to dominate
Whenever they can

Motherfucking animals
Unholy mesomorphs
The way we treat our fellow man is crazy
The way we treat our mother Earth
Is a kind of suicide

How can anyone keep mute?
But to speak of it means death for me
And worse resurrection

All I want from life now Is freedom
Perhaps a bit of peace

To walk the beach
Though it will be without you
To express myself in anyway
It feels right to do
But for the spoken word
I've had my fill of conversation
Loathe to add to the cosmic noise
But I can dream
To live with you
And watch our children grow

But were you ever completely mine?
Or was your heart too young and wild
Too full of wanting
To belong to anyone?
Not ownership
It's commitment that I mean
The unconditional giving of one's heart

In the end I think you fell in love with an idea
As if it was a dream
I'm not the last of the Mohicans
Just a man is all
You put me on a pedestal
From which you had to know
I would someday fall

The I you thought you saw
Was not the I I am or was
I was bound to disappoint you
I think I may have known it then
I did not say a thing

I was never good enough
You were too good to be true
What was a man like me
Doing with a woman like you?

2014 / 2017 / 2020 / 2021 / 2022

ONCE UPON A TIME AND THEN (HONEYMOON)

The westerly trades blew the clouds up
The first day of our honeymoon
But I was blind to these pretensions
Inside the beached bungalow
We were busy making love

You would think
I would have known enough
To know

Life is a dynamic thing
Nothing stays the same for long
But at that time I could not see
The coming of the hurricane

When one's wildest dreams come true
Like mine did with you
It's so easy to lose touch
With what we call Reality
That week
(Or was it more?)
Was up to then the best time of my life
But then every day with you
Was better than the one before

Until the sky fell down on us
Until I lost it all
The money
Our good name

But none of it
Mattered much to me
He giveth and he taketh away

I thought I could live with anything
Arrogant as Hell
Until the storm blew black
And ravaged us

And worse by far
I lost you along the way

2014 / 2017 / 2020 / 2021 / 2022

WHEN THE HOWLING STOPS

Hellhounds and the moon's minions
Feast on living bones
And drink the blooded wine of those
Without the spirit or the will
Or (God help them)
The strength to endure

Defenseless hopeless people
Suffering
The low hanging fruit in Satan's orchard
On which the Devil feasts
Unafraid of God's admonishings
A thorn in God's side

But the moon's the same
When the howling stops
It lights the ways of evil ones
As well as saints
It shines it's countenance on love

The night is magic
When the moon is full

And the sky is home to the multitudes
Seventeen billion trillion stars
In the vastness

Light years apart

The gentle sea breeze
Blows the shim aside
Miles low on the radio
The breaking waves
The ocean's lullabies

I sense your longing
Your breathing
The way you do when you get that way
To leave no doubt of your desire

I'm still surprised
Every time you want me
The miracle of love

The soft skin inside you
When I turn you over
The rivulets of sweat run
To the hollows of your arching back

I am
For now
A mortal man
A failed one at that
But once I was blessed
To have lived and loved with you
My only angel

The Goddess of my wildest dreams

2014 / 2017 / 2020 / 2021 / 2022

THE COLOR OF THE STARS

Cornered
All thought out
I have no more ideas
Ready to surrender but I won't
I don't roll that way
My bed is made
I'll sleep in it
If need be to the end of the world or me
Covered by the irony
That covers all of us

The higher one climbs
The farther the fall
Cushioned by belief
If it is at all

If there is time after this
And if I still have the strength
I will rise again to climb above
The highest height
I reached before the fall
To find another mountain
Even if it's twice as tall

For all I learned in this falling
Will make it that much easier to stand
Against the gales that blow
Where the air is thin and clear enough
To finally see the color of the stars

It's only fear that can obscure the view
And the noises in one's head up there
That so often confuse

So don't think too much
Never look down
Take heart
Look and be still
Experience

For up here where the air is thin
The winds of change blow rapidly
Dangerous to those caught dreaming
Or otherwise ill-prepared
Like a sudden storm on Everest
Can do a climber in

If he survives
He will find
There is much more work to do
So many other mountains
Left to climb

Judge me
If you are perfect
Or if you dare
For the best of us are sometimes sinners
And the worst of us are sometimes saints
We are evil
We are holy
We are Human after all

2014 / 2017 / 2020 / 2021

THE INHERITANCE

Hell takes on all comers
Satan sends no one away
Never discriminates
Like the Lord does at Saint Peter's gates
When we stand before him
To ask his permission
To pass through to the radiance

In Satan's realm all are welcome
To come and burn for eternity
Even Satan's fires require fuel
The worst sinners
The fallen saints
The almost good enough
To pass through the pearly gates

And every now and then
For reasons of their own
Some will choose Hell
As their eternal home
Maybe the one they loved in life is there
Could be they are angry with the Lord

Suffering through a life of constant testing
And all the years of yearning
And unanswered prayers
The almost unbearable pain

Should I have that choice to make
I'd choose the place that you will be
Out of place as I may be in Heaven
But not so much
As you would be in Hell
There are no angels there
But for the fallen one

The leaders of a revolution
Meant to change the status quo
Risk disgrace and worse
Often losing everything
Quieted or dead
Banished or encaged
Or in a coffin laid

Woe to those of whom
The people speak of well
Like their fathers did
Of prophets they killed

In the end
No matter who we are
We must work out our own salvation

I write these words
Unlikely ever to be read
I make paintings by the dozen
Unlikely to be seen
I venerate the actual

Painters and poets
Our prophets and our sages

And though I tried
I mean I gave my all
It surprises me
I still continue to make art
If anybody should know better
It is I

The Earth groans beneath the tons of shit
Made in the name of art
Forests felled for the stuff to make it with
All this garbage makes it hard to tell
If there are any among those who try
Who make it well

But I go on
In spite of all
I must
So let others make their work
I will make my own

The Rich men build high their walls of sin
And the cynical are always weak
They talk too fucking much
While those subject to Quixotic dreams
Suffer great ridicule

The people are embarrassed and afraid
Of the righteousness of dreamers
And of holy fools
So they put an end to them

Drowning in tears of sorrow
Their eyes dimmed with age

Sailing now
On serene seas
Even if against the wind

In the storm
They turn with the gales
The winds and raging waves behind them
Riding like The Big Kahuna
In order to survive

Left to wonder what went wrong
And why
Then to pray for Judgment Day

When for their many sins
The evil ones will reap their just rewards
And the meek will finally gain
Their inheritance

2014 / 2017 / 2020 / 2021 / 2022

MYSTERY ROAD

The heavy waved Atlantic rolled
The steel gray
The northeast gales
Made mad water music
The big blow stoked the spray

The tide was low enough
So there was still some sand to stand on
Wrapped against the weather
I walked out into it

Wishing and hoping can be poisonous
And most often useless anyway
Other than the misery they cause

We might as well walk down
That mystery road
Hit our knees and pray
In the end another test of faith

All this really hurts
And certain silences are the loudest screams
When one's love is mute
When there is nothing left to say

Time lies heavy on the heart
Hungry for Truth
A heart that desires work
With sacred fire

All of us are linked to life
By all of our past livings
Some say our instincts
Are the captains of our fate

The lines of life are thin in many places
Like the ones between love and hate
Life and death
Fame and infamy

The history of those things already done
Differ much in their subjectivity
The Truth is there
But hard work will be required
For it to be revealed

2014 / 2017 / 2020 / 2021 / 2022

LAST NIGHTS

The last night
I spent with my father
Miami Beach
Collins Avenue
Before it became so chic
A place near The Eden Rock
The Montmartre Hotel

He had come to visit me at school
But looking back
It seems to me he made the trip
To say goodbye
For he knew that when he left me
He would go away to die

That night he spent coughing
Awake all night
A symptom
Of his advanced heart disease
He thought I was asleep
I guess he didn't want to bother me
I did what I thought I should
I pretended not to hear him

I've never been so fucking scared
Much more for his death
That we both knew was coming
Than I will be for my own

O Pop
Forgive me please
For not putting you to bed
Since that night
(A half century ago)
There has been no moment
I haven't been afraid

Next morning
He made it seem he was OK
So I acted that way too
The way you face your mortality
Should be
Completely up to you

We said goodbye

No big deal
I would see him soon

Two weeks later
In his coffin laid
One last chance to look on him
Before they closed the lid
Every day since then
I thank the Lord
For he was my father
I will always be his kid

But to my youngest boys
I'm an old fool and worse
I guess right now
They need to do
What it is they need to do
Circumstances being what they are
Who can blame them ?

Life is hard
One day perhaps
They'll understand
Who I was
Who I am
What I did and did not do
And why
What they mean
And meant to me
We've been apart since we said goodbye
July 2010

In all that I have so far lost
The thing that hurts by far the most
Is the loss of all of you
I pray my boys will never dream of me with regret
The wasted time
The things we've left unsaid
But boys are not yet men
And meant to be that way

The last night I spent with you
An old house
We slept above the covers

To the extent we slept at all

Neither one of us had a lot to say
But we cried our share of tears
That last night
Before the day
They buried me alive

2014 / 2020 / 2021 / 2022

OCTOBER'S PAGE
(THE CALENDAR)

The walls liver red
A play of greens
The turquoise ceiling
Like the waiter's hair
And he is wearing white
The pool table
An antique even then
The naples yellow floor

Shapes of different people
A vision of the human lean
A table of seduction
A solitary man well in his cups
Two old men
Share drunken secrets
Beneath the gas lights' glow

Color sharded aureoles
Twelve thirteen
The morning of another day
So near
To the artist's final one

Vincent died of loneliness
A holy soul
Full of love for everyone
Alone but for His brother
Who in the end
Lived too far away

2014 / 2017 / 2020 / 2021

BAD DREAMS AND GOOD

Another ugly day outside today
The Brabant sky
Coal miner gray

But no matter how bad it gets
It's nothing like a day
In those places we make war
It rains steel and lead and fire there
The clouds bring death and destruction
Instead of rain

The whirlwind whips the sands of Babylon
The Reaper reaps away
The money-men do Satan's business
And say it's for the U.S.A.

For the lucre and the kind of fame
They earn
By killing children
For their profit in our name

Given a choice
I'd rather share a meal
With the Dalton Boys
Or the brothers James

These are the days of shame
For they kill in anonymity
Droned death from the skies
Machines for which we pay
Run by adolescents
Ten thousand miles away

A video game
And they get paid
Ignorant
They know not
The price they'll pay
For their part
In the mayhem and the murder

Nowadays
It's hard to know exactly who we are
Why is it we feel so strange ?
Why is it we feel
Our own skins don't fit ?
Why are we so afraid ?

Perhaps because we somewhere know
How much we do not know

Humans are born to kill
Among all the other animals
We destroy
Just because we can

But even here I dream of better days

The harsh wind blew the clouds around
The leaves to mini-vortexes
Some hoovered high enough
To block the moonlight
The air was cold and crisp and clear
Ice crystals in December snow
The stars implored
A multitude
Seventeen billion trillion luminosities

Connect the dots for everything is written there
Surrounded by the sparkling
It was a night to wonder

Her gloved hand in my own
Our heart heated breath steaming
Hushed
Joined
We were then and Actual

And the tall trees silhouetted
The stars reflected on the iced pond
Down the hill
Across the dirt road
A magic night between
Christmas Day and New Year's Eve

There was no need to talk
For what was there to say
That we did not already feel?

The gusts set the clouds to dancing
To the wind music of the tallest trees
A woman and a man in love

As Actual as all that encompassed us
And the dome counterclockwise turned
The centered moon an oculus

I saw a band of angels in the sky
Uriel and Raphael
Michael on the Devil's neck
Gabriel
Blowing his fine horn
Flying in formation
Like they did around The Ark of the Covenant
On the way
When God brought the people out of Egypt

I did not ask if she saw them too
This was no time for talk
I prayed she did because for me
It was a glimpse of actuality
As actual as dreaming gets
Confronted by these cosmic Truths

Her face shined with an inner glow
And streaked with tears of joy
My face was too
Not the shine but the joyous tears
It was a dream
After all

I dreamt of sand dune fences
The weathered wooden ones
Rust red
Put there to gather sand
The gusts and gales blow around
To make mini mountains of the sand
To help keep the ocean's waves
From joining with the waters of the bay
In the hurricanes
That sometimes rush ashore
On my beloved island home

2014 / 2017 / 2020 / 2021 / 2022

HOSANA ON THE DAY

The sun and moon and stars
Extinguished
The ocean boiled
The water turned to blood
The rivers to the mountains ran
Instead of to the sea

Hunger now
Where yesterday
There was ample bread

The sun was painted black
A chariot of fire
Elijah and the angels sang
Hosana

The Lord was on His way

The gentle ones
Hide their eyes
Too meek to look
Afraid to run
Afraid to stay

On the fields of Armageddon
The battle coming
For at least five thousand years
In the end
Only the good enough
Will be left alive

Half of us will be destroyed
Sodom and Gomorrah like
But on a grander scale
One half
Of everyone this time
Of the eight billion souls on Earth
Four billion disappear

Judgment Day

In the end the good will rule
And sinners will finally get
What we have so long deserved

                    2014 / 2020 / 2021 / 2022

DONAHUE'S

In the gray of a false dawn
The penetrating fog
Opaque and wet and chill
The beach blurred in mist
Muffled sound
Like when it snows
But for the water
And even then a little bit

The gulls peck at broken Horseshoe Crabs
Their holy carapace
Abandoned at low tide
Prehistoric
Beach scum and kelp
A million shells

I thought of you
Those ridiculous riding pants
You would wear when we first met
And that multicolored woolen poncho
You bought
On some trip you took
To Peru or Mexico

We would see a film
And then to Donahue's
You introduced me to Martinis there
Martinis and Sardines

I walked to the water's edge
Dreaming
But the tide turned
And the fog was finally broken

I was wakened from this reverie
By the misty sun
And the surge of the sea

The angels sing before the lord
Holy harmonies
The light shines
On those of us
With eyes
Clear enough to see
Ten years ago

The brightest it would ever be

Suddenly the darkness
Some things I guess
You never get over
Like the death of a great love
The end of you and me

Come kiss my tears
My only love
It is my time to fly away
You are finally free of me
But all my vows
Are as they were
Even if your love is gone

Come
Say goodbye to me
My life's love
My once best friend

I'm dying
Like some hero in a twisted play
A comic tragedy
Yet now that it is almost over
I am strangely satisfied
With all the loss

Life has done OK by me

2014 / 2017 / 2020 / 2021 / 2022

COLD SUNS AND RAINLESS CLOUDS

Please tell me what to call this feeling
On the dark side of wicked woe
And far beyond despair
But worst of all it's getting so
I no longer care
Though feeling pain is the only way
To be certain I'm alive in here

No man should give up
On those beliefs
He holds most dear
Even for a woman's love
Whom he is mad about

I guess she shouldn't want him to
But women can be selfish in that way
And anyway who can know
What a woman really wants ?
A woman's heart a labyrinth
A massive maze of contradiction

Dreaming is a perfect kind of poetry
Fundamental to the soul
For the Human Soul requires nourishment
Art is the food it needs

Poets in denial
Are committing spirit suicide

The money-men call us
Romantic fools
They want us to forget
Poetry exists
To learn another trade
One that will pay our bills
And more important theirs

To live the way they want us to
Defies the way it is
We betray our own hearts
If we do
Guilty of soul treason
In the first degree

False promises
Are cold suns
Unrealized dreams
Are rainless clouds
Form without substance is nowhere
Unless the substance is the form

Broken hearts can kill

But lost love
Is the hardest thing
Like death
There is no coming back from it

The best one can hope for
Is freedom
To do creative work
After that to die in peace

Relieved
That it's all over

2014 / 2017 / 2020 / 2021 / 2022

MISPLACED

I misplaced the lines
I wrote yesterday
And for my life I can't recall
What it is I had to say
But I'm sure the better part of it
Had to do with you
Like the better part of all I think and dream
The part that's not concerned with death
It seems I am obsessed by you
And The Reaper Man

Maybe I wrote of Saturn's moons
Perhaps the Morning Star
But it's far more likely
I wrote
Of how beautiful you are

Could be I wrote about the war we waged
To save the children's lives
Maybe I wrote of your Gaelic Eyes

One thing for sure I'm getting old
At my age one forgets a lot
But there are some things I can't forget
Most of them concerned with you

You were the queen of my happiness
The sovereign of my heart
The mother of my youngest boys
The light
The air I breathed

With you I dwelled in Paradise
Now I hang my hat in Hell

I must have written a line or two
About the darkness of my days
Of the endless nights

I may have wondered when I died
If there would be anyone to mourn me
Perhaps to say a word or two
On my behalf
Perhaps my kids will cast my bones into the sea

Could be I wrote
Of the idea of the Ideal

2014 / 2017 / 2020 / 2021 / 2022

THE BALLAD OF JOE SMITH

A young man walks the beach alone
He screams his most private thoughts
To the sea
Knowing they will be swallowed up
By the sound of the crashing waves
The perfect place to try out new ideas
A way to experiment
While holding on to self-esteem
A great place for the thinking man
A lovely solitude

But here in Hell the walls have ears

The next time you watch the waves roll in
Think of each as a man's idea

I'm filled with things I dare not say
Until the day I'm set free
To tell them once again
To the sea

To think of all the ways I hurt
Makes this unbearable
The demons that come to party
Begin to get the best of me

And even if it's true
I'm no longer loved by those
I love the most
What good will it do
To say things I do not mean?
It only makes it that much worse

They must believe my spirits
Are much better than they are
That my heart is protected
Impervious to pain

React in anger
Deflect the blame
Invent scenarios neither false nor true

I'll have to wait to try to put
The egg together
Again
But it's only love I feel for you and them

If there is to be a broken heart
Better mine than yours
I deserve it anyway
If one of us most suffer
It's the least I can do
But still it hurts like Hell
Life plays out
The way it will

Each of us
Have many questions
Forever left unanswered
And for some
A shit-load of great regret

A soldier
Call him Joe
Walking point on patrol in 'Nam
1968

If I see Charley
I'm gonna blow his ass away
Before he does it to me

But it's so strange
They will have me kill a Human Being
Or two or more
They tell me that's what I'm here for
But they never tell me why
And I will never know the names of those I kill

But I know back home
Ralphie is the corner deli-man
Sal the barber cuts my hair
James the kid who mows the lawn
Is not ending another's life
More personal?

Here I am a jungle-man
Set to kill some mother's son
I've never met
And I've no idea what he has done
To deserve it
I guess that's meant to make it easier

It's war they say
And war is dirty business
But what is it to a man
When you take his life away?
What is it in the eyes of God?

It's a person whom they've ordered me to kill
Not some abstract thing
Each time I do what I am told
I kill a part of my soul as well
The best part of me

Hello my name is Smith
Joe Smith
Isn't it a shame
One of us has got to die?
Isn't it a shame
They order us to kill?
Is it not an abomination
Before any God?

You may hate my country
And you may well have reason to
But it's me
You're about to kill

What un-Godly games
They order us to play
What a fucking shame we play them

Anyway
I've had enough
I'm gonna throw my gun away
And you can do whatever
It is you're going to
But when you do
I beg of you

Remember my name

2014 / 2017 / 2020 / 2021 / 2022

REVOLUTION TIME

The masses scream for change
Like they almost always do
While they look around
For the first good man to kill

A diversion and an entertainment

They hunt other human beings
Like they were deer
Allowed by their masters
Those who keep their leashes on
To release them for a little while
When they think they need the exercise

The savages who make the rules
Set standards
For what passes as their decency
They regulate
The way we are supposed to behave
They do this for all kinds of reasons
For money mostly
And to maintain the status quo

These maniacs won't stand for failure
And less for disobedience
They marry within their families
To keep the money there

The weak they won't abide
They send them away to die
The thinning of the herd
Their hearts have holes in them
If they have hearts at all

And they are in so many other ways
Incomplete

Social misfits with their own kind
An insulated chain of money-men
In other words a bunch of boors
With overblown opinions of themselves

These guys seem healthy
But their souls are sick
Often filled with anguish and despair

Or it may be that every one of them
Is clinically insane

It's easier for the psychopath
To flourish economically
In this sick society
Than those concerned
With the condition of The Human Soul

They swear allegiance to those things
They think they believe
They know nothing about empathy or loyalty
They act the role of an aristocrat
From the fifteenth century
But they have not a bit of class
Conventional in how they think
(those of them who think at all)
And they are very strange
In the ways they behave

They would rather spend their time
Staring at their balance sheets
Than *The Mona Lisa*
Read the *Wall Street Journal*
In lieu of *Moby Dick*

They are cold blooded
Hard of heart
Stiff of neck
Severe in their self-righteousness
Their lack of self-awareness often dangerous

But the worm will turn
Like it always has
When it's time for turning

Soon it will be light again
For those I love and me
But when it is we would be wise
To temper our joy

For eventually the darkness
Will once again
Like a curtain fall
The end of another act in the play

The way things work
All there is is love and change
Once true love is lost
It's horrible hard to find again

Here I play the Devil's advocate

Suppose the guy
Who shot two cops to death
Cold blooded on a Brooklyn street
As they sat in their patrol car
Suppose he was not crazy
Like they want us to believe?

What if he saw them
Not as cops
But as soldiers
In the uniform of his mortal enemy?
Soldiers in the army of the money-men
Heroes of the status quo

These guys who wore the same uniform
As those who killed that kid in Ferguson
As those who kneeled on George Floyd's neck
Who killed Eric Garner
Both shouting I can't breathe
One of them calling for his mother

The cops paid a pittance for their work
Not to protect and save
The things that well-meaning cops
Think they're paid to do
But to enforce the laws written to ensure
The money stays with the money-men
The status quo is maintained
Ninety five percent of everything
Goes to the five percent of them

Suppose the killer of these cops believed
Saving his country
Required massive rapid violent change
Time to get down to it
Time to make war

Power to the people !
Good Lord
It's revolution time !

Suppose the killer of these cops
Was logical and rational
In other words perfectly sane
Acting on his beliefs
Inspired by a certain group of timely facts
Like Adams and Franklin were
Like Washington and Jefferson
Like the minutemen at Lexington
And those at Bunker Hill

There is no reason that justifies
The taking of another life

The innocent too often killed
In any war
We see it in the middle east
Where fire rains down on children
In our name

The time has come
When we must decide the side we'll choose
When the shit hits the fan
And the lead begins to fly

One man's killer
May be a hero to another

It's not the righteous who write our histories
But the servants of the winners of our countless wars
Paid to write them by the powerful
On the winning side

History has become a point of view.

2014 / 2017 / 2020 / 2021 / 2022

AFTER ALL

The only thing I feel
Is sad today
Can't shake it off
Can't make it go away
Beyond the point of talking
I've nothing much to say
I struggle mightily
To get through this
Another awful day

What do other people
Do about the pain ?

Some find relief
At the bottle's bottom
Some shoot it
Through a vein
I used to find it walking
On the beach
In the rain

But hold your grief
It's the ways of the world
That need to change
And the meek and innocent
Who need our sympathy

There are times
I find some humor knowing
How far and fast
A man can fall
I'm here in Hell
After all

But not today
The time has come
The judges will be judged
The good will be set free
Judgment Day

I lost count of the stars
Never mind the days
So many things I believed I saw
Were never there to see

I heard Heavenly music
I hit my knees to pray
Now I don't believe
The music I heard
Was ever played

I saw the Chama
Running red as blood
The Sangre de Cristo Mountains
Painted blue
Holy mother full of grace
Could it be it's all a dream ?

Spiritus Sanctus
Save the saints
His time has come

And tomorrow
If I still live
And if you are still there
I will find you
If you want me to
To try to get it right this time
And after all

2014 / 2020 / 2021 / 2022

SPEAKING OF THE SOUL

It's as if I was put in here to see
If life on Earth
Was still a possibility
And it's looking very grim
From where I sit

I've been tried
And I've failed
But it ain't over
Until it is
There is some little more life in me

Why is it that people need to hurt one another
When it's so easy to make them glow?

Thin of soul
Wanting heart
Craving money
Embracing greed
Jonesing out on the need for speed
At an enormous cost to all of us
In the wholesale loss of quality

So take your math
And shove it
I'm speaking of the soul!
Nourish yours
If you have one still

Their technology
Will destroy
The Human Heart

The math they know is just enough
For them to count their money
But they don't know
And never will
One plus one rarely equals two
No matter what
They've been taught in school
Or what it says on their computing machines

They stultify with the internet
They deal in false imaginings

Like Disneyland
And Disney does
You pay
Through the nose
To be exposed to their ideas
In the movies and T.V.
Disneyland was not enough
So like God they made a world

And that rat-fuck-big eared rodent Mickey
Is just another stinking vermin louse
A fucking Hitler youth
There is a certain kind of death
In their animations

Call me mad if you must
But I've never been so sane
Or saw the Truth so clearly
Yet somehow it saddens me

Some hearts
Like my own I guess
Were meant to spend their days
Overcoming
All kinds of shit
Always searching
For something to feel good about

But you know that things aren't going well
When the best that can be said
Is it could be worse

I guess that is to be expected
When one spends their life
Trying to attain
The unattainable
For heartache is a certainty
When you chase the White Whale

2014 / 2017 / 2020 / 2021 / 2022

THE LIE

The vortex counterclockwise swirled the Maelstrom
A hole in the sea
Like Ismael I watched
As all I owned was lost to me
In the fathomless depths
Where countless sailors sleep

I was saved
Condemned to mourn
Death would have been a mercy
Prevented all the pain

It's been years
Since I was locked away in here
Where no one cares to see the cruelty
The suffering that results from being buried alive
Made to watch my loved ones lives' unfold
Like some kind of TV show

But it is dark in here
And difficult to see
Anyway
To die for love is beautiful

Certain secrets
Can not be revealed
Which leads to a heavy kind of loneliness
But love needs not the kind of understanding
That must be put down in words

We strive for our beliefs

Contentment is but a kind of sleep
A sign of approaching death
But birth is no beginning
As death is not an end

It's only transformation

I fear those things I can't ignore
Or laugh away

To know what's on the other side
When the swirling stops
And the vortex dies
And The Maelstrom disappears

We are motes in the light of the stars

Freedom may be finally found
In the vastness of space
Luminous and gorgeous
And time as we know it
Obsolete

So what is there to fear on Earth?
And pain is just a point of view
That comes of how we deal with one another
But dust feels no pain
And even seekers have the time for longing

But when the pictures stop
And in the peace and the silence
The questions end
We will know at last
The great simplicity
And discover what we thought we knew
There is only change

So let us laugh at Death
Like O'Neill's Lazarus
For each one brings an end to a cycle of suffering
Born to die and gratefully
But never to Death
The rest is slavery
For no one is free while they live

O how we strive to find a bit of Truth
And short of that create our own illusions
Each life a carnival ride
A work of fiction
A motherfucking lie

For what can we know of Truth
Yet some of us will never stop
Seeking it

Like Ahab his leviathan

2014 / 2017 / 2020 / 2021 / 2022

THE HOLY TRAIN

At my old age
Some sit down to write
The guest list for their funerals
To pick the music to be played
To figure out what they want
The eulogy to say
And whom they want to say it
But that kind of thing is not for me

Just wrap me up
Throw me in the raging waters
When the tide changes
In Reynold's Channel
That connects the ocean to the bay
Separates Jones Beach
From our island's eastern end

Maybe after
Stop into the Patio
If it still exists
Knock back a drink or two
And if you would
Hit your knees and pray
I can use the help up there
For I have heard that righteous prayer
Paves the way
Through Heaven's gates

But while we live
We all know fear
We are wounded from time's torture
We shed too many tears

All of us are terrified
And many crazy
We must keep our souls fit
Be ready when that holy train
Rolls 'round the bend
To hop on board and joyously
Whenever it arrives

An angel of The Lord
Drives that train
And angels don't deal with time
The way we do
They mess not with things like hours or days

Death is Death
When the dying's done

So right your wrongs
Come to terms with your regrets
If you are able
Express your love to those you're closest to
Be prepared
For when you least expected
That holy whistle's gonna to blow

I dreamed about those times
I bought flowers for you
Four dozen roses
Sometimes more
You'd give me hell for my extravagance
But I knew you loved them just the same
From my deepest soul I loved you then

The kind of love that never ends

We danced slow dances to songs of love
Old records before your time
I held you close
We clung hard to the love we made

O honey
What a time that was !
The best of my life by far
It brings me joy to remember
But also a great deal of pain
You were mine
I let you down
I know I am to blame

You are so exquisite
In a Botticelli kind of way
But in certain moods you become
Like Gardner and Bacall
A sexy stylish dame
A Raymond Chandler kind of frail
A smoldering spy
Difficult to fully figure out

A mystery I could never solve
But God knows how I tried

In the end I guess
I got it wrong
It was too damned hard
To get my head around

What appeared to be the Truth
Was actually a clusterfuck
I've yet to find the strength to face

I'm far from a holy man
And for all the perfect things you are
Nobody's perfect

The sinful often think
They are wiser than they are
They scheme and lie and play their games
Holier than thou
Their hypocrisy a crying shame

I believe their lack of heart
Their unwillingness to forgive
Are symptoms of their own sinning
The product of their damaged souls
As if in forgiving
They would give themselves away

The Lord forgives
All who ask sincerely
But some of us are too afraid
To do the same

Forgiveness
Can only come from God
Anyway
Flawed creatures
Who are we to forgive ?
Everyone connected
In our shared
Imperfect Humanity

There are wounds of longstanding
That never really heal
That In the moments of remembering
Bring us instantly to tears

It may be the best Man can do
Is face it
To take life on the chin
To learn to better cope
With its multitudinous uncertainties
And ambiguities

We all compose our own sweet songs
Of love and loss
And forgetting
Is one way to deal
With heartbreak

We walk around terrified
And act as if our terror makes us wise
I can no longer make much sense of it
From behind these weary eyes
After living in this place for years
Where everyone's a sinner
And everything's
A lie

2014 / 2017 / 2020 / 2021 / 2022

PREHISTORIA

It takes a gentle spirit
To heal a Human Heart
But there are not enough of them
To go around
I mean the healers
Not the Heartbreak
God knows there's plenty of that
More die of it every year
Than Cancer
A lousy way to disappear

It's the longing that puts one at risk
And lost love
Leads to despondency
And while I'm certain
It's better to have loved and lost
It doesn't mean it's easy
Or that I'm strong enough to handle it

The rate of change has metamorphosized
From modern man to prehistoria
Things are changing faster
Than man has ever known

Antediluvian modernists
We are much more like our aped fathers
Than the men we will never know
I mean our children's children
Or maybe not
Until their own or theirs

For time has folded
And tomorrow
All our yesterdays
Twenty thousand years of change to come
In this century

Still primitive
Like Cro-Magnon Man

We kill in wholesale lots
When eighteen year old boys and girls
In hollowed mountains
Sit and play
In Virtual reality

But actual children actually die
And these teenage droners
Have to live with it
They take it to their graves

State sanctioned blessed
The lee side of Truth
Ten thousand miles away
Sheltered from their crimes
And from the pain
They caused

Inside their hollowed mountain fort

We are before civilized
More barbaric
Than the wildest fiercest jungle beasts
Who at least are nourished by
The animals
They kill to eat

2014 / 2017 / 2020 / 2021 / 2022

SILENT FLASHES

The soft breeze from the east northeast
The way it is this time of year
A humid afternoon
Spending time horizon watching
Where the sky and the ocean meet
Looking for the masted ships
That cut the line
To make the poor man's scale

The sky lit in silent flashes
Still too far to hear the thunder
I watch the storm roll in
Counting seconds in between
The gorgeous luminosities

On the beach
We measure time and distance that way
Twelve seconds to the mile

And it seems as if the best loved of us
Are rebel angels
Who fight against all odds for their beliefs
In the end they finally win
Like the good rarely do on Earth
Though often too late for them
Jesus Christ
Mozart
Martin and Abraham
Vincent and Che
Gandhi
Malcolm X
J and RFK

The sky an exhibition
A contrast of dark and light
The western sky is blood
Weightless

But to the east the sky portends

Deep violet now to black sappy green
And the flashes now but twelve seconds between
The storm a mile away

Like Turner tied to a ship's mast
To experience the storm
I bear witness

I sit bedoomed on the beach
Sky colors changing
I listen
To what the wise wind has to say

It was you who saved me from myself
I would have stayed
In the middle
Of the thunder and the lightning
The roar the flash
The wicked waves and roiled seas
Overtopping the dunes
Meant to keep the tide away
And from mixing with the now wild waters of the bay

And it seems as if
The best loved of us
Are rebel angels
Who fight against all odds for their beliefs
And in the end they finally win
Like the good rarely do on Earth
Though often too late for them
Jesus Christ
Mozart
Martin and Abraham
Vincent and Che
Gandhi
Malcolm X
J and RFK

2014 / 2017 / 2020 / 2021 / 2022

DOUBLED DOWN

Nightmares carried through the days
Intense ponderings
The forked flames
And lightnings shout
Betailed devils beckon me
To leap down among them

Like Laertes
His sister's grave

Symptoms of my manic intensities
My art is my White Whale
No time to sleep
No patience for that kind of dreaming

By surrendering
To this great purpose
I pit myself against
Gods and Devils both
In other words I'm stuck
In my own way of being
Doubled down
Self-inflicted creativity

A vulture
Drawing
On my hungry heart
Feeding
On my blood
Stripping me
Of my vitality
I mean those times
I don't feel
Like the mighty
Kong

2015 / 2017 / 2020 / 2021 / 2022

KING

The seer sees
The poet feels
The prophet foretells
Hearts stirred
Souls profoundly moved

Pondering
The misery and grief
Surrounding them
And all of us

Imagination fails
Actuality becomes too actual

We strain to hear the thoughts of God
And Hell and eternity
The talk is talk
But talk is cheap
And the study of the human heart
Comes dear

The light
Out of the darkness leaps
But the dark ones leap
Out of the light as well

Promises are mercilessly broken
The breakings more than agony
And more than woe
They stab and burn
They destroy the soul

Of those
Who still believe the one they love
When she said forever and I do
Black is the day
I lived to say goodbye to you

There is no end to this misery
The broken trust the thing
Betrayed
Mistakes are often made in times of tragedy

Alone
I crossed the stars
I once so loved
I live
Mostly in the darkness now
A resident of Hell

Like sweet Jesus I begin to doubt
But I'm not the king of anything
I'm my earthly father's sinful son
Is all
And unless you are the son of God
Death is death when the dying's done
No matter who you are
No matter who you think you are

But Jesus walked on water
Made the blind to see
The lame to walk
He cured those with Leprosy
So long as those who asked of him
Believed

Miracle maker
Jesus suffered for the rest of us
Actual nobility
The King Of The Jews

Resurrected

The rest of us stay dead
When it's death we do

2015 / 2017 / 2020 / 2021 / 2022

DANCE

He puts his boy beneath the coverlet
She made for him
He kisses him good night
After the boy finishes his prayers

His hot grief breath
Smells of tobacco and alcohol
Which would kill the father in the end
But not that night
And not for years

The boy lay still
To hear his father climb the stairs
To his dying mother's room

Father O'Brien's there
The local priest
The boy is old enough to understand
His mother is dying
Not long for this world

But she was never at ease with life when hale

An angel in a sinner's paradise
A fish out of water
Unprepared
For the mayhem
In living any Human life
The perfect mother
The perfect wife

Too good to last for long
In this hard-hearted world
A saint among degenerates
Each unholy act was felt by her
A stab of pain
A fall from grace
Each sin
Another abomination

The boy pretends he's unaware
Something children do
For they rarely ask questions
They don't want to know the answers to
Something some

Never do outgrow
There are questions in this world unknown
Better left unanswered
His mother was going
The boy's first dance with Death

He hears his father weeping on the stairs
He had not before
Heard his father cry

His best friend is gone

In the heavy darkness of his room
The boy dresses and goes to him
Sometimes the boy is really
Father to the man

He finds his father in a chair
In the corner of the living room
Next to their Christmas tree
Not yet put away
Projected shadows from the fireplace
Paint the predawn walls
Like Indonesian puppets
A funereal fire dance

The boy dares not ask
Anyway he knows
The father takes his hand without a word
Pulls him close
They sit there in silence
Until the sun comes up

Another day another year
For every death at least one birth
He gives and takes away
At His own pleasure
So enjoy it when the music plays
And if you have the courage to
Remember

2015 / 2017 / 2020 / 2021 / 2022

HOME
(FOR RICHIE)

It's the calm before the storm
That's the most hideous
The gathering more awful
Than the gales
The danger more intense
Than the actual strife
The thought of death
Before dying

But life is war
And war is pain and hurt
And hate is woe
Obsession is the Devil's madness

I am a soldier of Fate
I do what I am told
Immutable
Set down the moment time began

I have fought my wars
Lived through the hurt and hate
But it is the wisdom gained
In the living on
That is the most wicked woe

Yet
We own our souls
Thus we are kings
Without them less than noble

Phosphorescent fires burn
Only white hot Hell remains
In the end no one can say
With integrity
I am the master
Of all that becomes of me

2015 / 2017 / 2020 / 2021 / 2022

MYSTIC DOORS

A man
Is not meant to dance
To another man's music
But be content to exist alone
Dancing to his own

To go to war
With anyone who would enslave him
To move away from the masses
And closer to belief

To own the courage
To walk through mystic doors
To move into eternity
To enter the unknown without fear
With an eager heart

We were young and foolish
Too damned full of ourselves
But we never did stop searching for the Truth
We cling to life
Old men now
Still flushed with the romance of illusion

But we must know
When we have been assailed
By the powers of darkness
No fool has ever won
A battle with the Devil for his soul
Without the help of God
I have suffered with my own intensely

Solitude if long enough
Will drive a soul to madness
The price we pay is the guilt we feel

There is nothing in the world more frightening
Yet uplifting too
Than a soul that dares
In the face of impossibility
A test of faith
The struggle is within ourselves
To be
Strong enough in our beliefs
To believe in the face of anything

2015 / 2018 / 2019 / 2020 / 2021 / 2022

RINGMASTER

I am beginning to distrust my work
My ambitions have been checked
Issues I believed
Were settled long ago
Certain philosophical positions
Dearly won
Are now in doubt

I used to be so sure
Where it was I stood
Something has tampered
With My equilibrium
Everything distresses me

I was the ringmaster
Of my own circus
A populizer
A liaison to the elite
Many people believed I had
What they were looking for

Subtlety for the subtle
Warmth for the cold
For the crude crudity
For the hypocrites hypocrisy
Atrocity for the atrocious
And always the best art

An Ivan the Terrible type
A would be Raskolnikov
Actors
And all other kinds of artists
Politicians
And want to be transgender men
A famous athlete passed his prime

More than a few Napoleons
A couple of Elvises
Many masters of the universe
Henry fucking Kissinger
A famous writer or two

Miles Davis
Who once told me
If your woman disappears
It only means the fuck is off
And a man needs to go out to find
Another bitch to get it on with

A Siberian Shaiman
A Hindu Swami
A rabbi or two
The Very Reverend James P. Morton
Nelson Mandela
General Tommy Franks
The Presidents of Iceland and Poland

United States Senators
Vice President Gore
The Dick Cheneys
I.M. Pei
The Kofi Annans
Vincent Price
And Saul Bellow

I must have been in the grip
Of some powerful electric force
And I was dangerous

I was bent too far
Bound to break
And now
Something has unbalanced me

There is a freedom that results in madness
And a freedom that comes of it
There are those who would rob me
Of the right to feel my agony
And suffer in my place
(Up to a point)

These motherfuckers must believe
They're so much higher than I am
Psychopaths
Acting
The part of saints
Boastful exhibitionists
Consumed by a certain kind
Of manic hypocrisy

They drive three hundred thousand dollar cars
Then pretend to be radical
They talk the talk
Promoting the destruction
Of the affluent society
To which they belong

I know
I was one of them

For each speech they give they're paid
Two hundred fifty grand
People of deep convictions?
Give me a fucking break!
Sour grapes?
Probably

One sad thing follows another
In this place
One hears grotesque stories
And abominations
Gothic tales but so much darker
And worse they are real
These unholy things
Man does to man
There's no other animal
Capable of this kind of malice

Man is mad

Though old
I still question
Every fucking thing
Dear Lord please
Bring me peace
Relieve me
Of this heavy burden

2015 / 2020 / 2021 / 2022

ANIMALS

This is not the Amazon
Where in wait
Anacondas lay
This is not the Barbary
There are no pirates from Cathay
No far east jungle this
As far as I know
There are no wild tigers roaming here
Central Park
New York, New York
U.S.A.

The animals are a different sort
More ferocious
More dangerous
More mean

They masquerade
In the form of Man
Hide amongst the foliage for their prey
Amongst the dirty needles
Used prophylactics
And rats the size of dogs

Shylocks and Mob Boys
Dealers in happy dust
Hungry cannibals are everywhere
Ready to eat
You and yours
After
They have finished with theirs

2015 / 2021

BEWILDERED AND REPELLED

Some fear freedom
Like the plague
They cry out
For the chains of tyranny
If nothing else it means
Man has thus far failed

Terrified
At the thought
Of deciding for ourselves
We only understand oppression
We lust after it
The tyrant's foot upon our necks

The things we hate the most
Are freedom and responsibility
Loath to take any kind of risk
To face the choices of the Universe
With the courage that demands

To stand up for the way it is
With a stout and open heart
With the requisite humility
To hit our knees from time to time
And pray

Bewildered and repelled
By our own powers
Unable to understand ourselves
Trapped between the flesh and spirit
The body and the soul
The struggle heaps and cripples us
Never good enough
Not worthy

If one looks hard enough
The ordinary becomes magic
There's more relief in illusion
Than a double shot of Jack

One can dream of getting right again
One can dream of resurrection

Like Christ
Who died between two criminals
We are surrounded by vice

Sometimes current calamities
Are blessings dressed up
Trouble has a sweetness of its own
It eats the status quo

I am still waiting for the time
The boy gives birth to the man
I've spent my life
Trying to be
Nothing ever stops
It divides and multiplies

Ground to dust
But
It does not get blown away
Not those things between lovers
Not between real friends

In the end we will all compose
Our own sweet songs
Of death and failure

Selective Amnesia
A way to deal with heartbreak

And Death the salesman never ceases
Going door to door
Dealing with all of us
When the time comes
All sales final
Justice achieved
The end of the beginning
Again

2015 / 2018 / 2020 / 2021 / 2022

THE PRICE PAID TO SING

Lucid in certain moments
An unexpected marvelous
Completely unpredictable clarity
Like when art fights its way out of shit

O poets and painters
Protectors of the arts
Is your love of it some kind of joke?
A sexual expedient?
An excuse to sleep outside beneath
The vaulted starry firmament?

There must have been a time
With your fantastic pride
(Though better you were chaste and humble)
When you were on the top of the world
When you had your feet on the neck of princes
When you had fame and wealth and influence
While you reveled in man's fateful folly
Playing wild games with unholy lovers
Making them crawl

When you ruined others' husbands
For the fun of it
You flung away human lives
Like fistfulls of sand
The Tsarina of a country full of sycophants
Until you lost your mind

No one man
Was enough for you
You wanted to make love with the Universe
But the Universe recoiled from you
To the Universe
You were like the rest of us
Less than a grain of sand

Art is not the copy of nature
Or anything the artist sees
The artist's job is to manifest actuality
To pass it through his human heart

To turn it into art
All artists are poets
And all poets pay
For the songs they sing
Dearly

A poet must feel the Truth

Who would fuck around
When we pay so dear a price to make our music?

The money-men know how to look
But not how to see
An artist must see everything
Visible or not

The artist needs the courage to
Allow for accidents
That separates the great
From the good
To recognize what he can use
And throw the rest away

An artist must find the courage to fail
For that's the greater part of what we do
The question is how close we get
To the way it is

It's easy for men my age
To give up on worldly dreams
For his work
To believe
To tap into the Creative Force
That he knows is there
Like men at war in foxholes praying
There are no artist atheists

My vitality is proportionate
To the sensations that assail me
A longing
Nothing on Earth can satisfy

I hunger after things
I can not drink or eat
It is wisdom that I crave
And beauty
And love

I want to know
How to light the paint I use
To make the canvas shine
From the inside out
A broken off bit of Sun
To find a way to put the light in paint
Like Rembrandt did

There is a great and mighty joy in Heaven
For every sinner who repents
For Jesus gave his life for them

We search for a glimpse of God
For His hands we know are there
To hold our own
When we need it

We struggle
With the impossible
We seek the highest magic
With all the chaos and madness
We face in finding it

Never mind the fact
We are often terrified
And most of us are crazy

2015 / 2019 / 2020 / 2021 / 2022

BRAHMA BULL BAT OUTTA HELL

I ride this storm of life
Like a cowboy on a Brahma Bull
Moving like a motherfucking
Bat outta Hell
Nothing safe or secure
Everything in a state of change
Even the state of change is changing

I walk the high wire
Without a net
Like Rene Petite crossing St. John's dome
Never daring to look down on the abyss

In the off shore winds
That blow the water to mountains
The gulls guard the shore like sentinels
Until the waves break
Chasing everything in their way
Away

Yet some will ride their surfboards
On a tidal wave
The rest of us terrified
Run to the hills
To find the higher ground

The daring ones will attempt to do
Anything they can dream
Knowing
It's gonna end anyway

There's no escaping death
Each of us will meet The Reaper
We're playing with the house's money
We have nothing of our own to lose
When The Lord is ready He will call His loan
There's never been a Human Being who didn't pay

Dying young is relative
Be it thirty or one hundred years
Seventy years more or less is nothing to eternity
There's no reason for timidity
Let us give up
Our space on the wall
And dance
While we're still able

2015 / 2020 / 2021 / 2022

TESTS

Things play too hard with us
We are out of touch
With Nature
In other words
With the way it is

Even with God's miracles
One can not always like
The way the world is made
The hard way it treats you
Who would want to live again
To suffer life one more time around?

Even the Son of Man returned
To his father's breast
Even He had to die like a man
The price one pays for putting on his form

Even Jesus
Splendiferous
Even He who transformed the wickedness
Natural to Man
And showed us a more noble way to live

With all that He had to die
This lamb
This Son of Man
Even He had to die like a man

From the cross He cried
Confused by His father's will

God makes plans for the long haul
But we are short term animals
O but God is tough on us!

He tests us against the hardest rock
In the high heat of the hottest fire
To plunge us like a smithy
Into the coldest waters

Steel
Like Ahab with savage blood
Tempered his harpoon

He wants us new
Limber as a willow branch
Tough as leather
So that when we bend
(And we will bend)

To snap back
To dodge the bolts he throws at us
Quick minds quick feet
Nimble footed dancing

He gave us brains
With which to learn
To get what we need
To make due with what we have

To see when we look
Rather than to rely
On some other man's description
Of their own reality

Give Caesar what is his
But trust in God

No one knows the Truth
Or how best to live one's own
Much less an other person's life
There are no patents on Truth and love
Perfection is God's alone
We must learn to roll with the punches
Like Mohamed Ali
And like Bojangles dance
Copacetically
Keep to the rhythm
We will keep to life

God wants us strong

Man is the only animal
Who doesn't know at birth
All he will ever need to
And even when we think we know
We're very often wrong

It takes some time to learn enough to get it right
But only if we're lucky and we work for it
As long as a person wants to learn
They're too damned young to die

2015 / 2017 / 2020 / 2021 / 2022

FLIPSIDE

I lost my shadow
Yours grew twice as long
I thought of music
You sang the song
I washed my face
And you dried yours
I cried
You wiped away your tears

I was the B-side of a record
On which
The A-side is a masterpiece
A mega-hit
The B-side ignored
And very rarely played

Side-A's lady singer star
Never mind her name
Recently inducted
Into Heaven's Hall of Fame

The flipside of one another
Lovers
The best of friends
Husband and wife

But now
My life has devolved to this
On Fathers' Day

My shadow has been returned to me
A little more worn
The music has stopped
There are no more songs

I cry
Now more than ever
The tears are my own
And for me to wipe away
No longer lovers
No longer husband and wife
And now I fear
No longer even friends

There are great risks incurred
When you give your heart away
Love
A tightrope
Without a net
To catch you when you fall

A high wire act and I've fallen
A time or two before

But I have never fallen
As far and fast and hard as this
This is a fall
From which I shall not rise

Shattered like a piece of glass
My heart exploded

There is nothing to be done to ease the pain
I weep and groan and pace my cage
Lion like
Old and arthritic
Toothless and declawed

Reduced to this
Happy for my heart to stop
Yearning for death

How I miss your notched eyes
Your easy laugh
Remembering
Makes it worse

I need to put an end to it
But how can any man
Much less a man like I
Make himself numb ?
I need to feel to make my art
Like I need to breathe to live

I would like to paint my sadness
Make a painting in a minor key
To testify
To whatever of the Truth
I've been blessed
To experience and see

2015 / 2018 / 2019 / 2020 / 2021 / 2022

GAUZY

I've never had a great hold
On actuality
But the little I have slips away
The line between fiction and Truth
Gauzy

It exhilarates
To know death is near

If one succeeds in one place
He likely fails in another
Is it art you want to make
Or is money?

Too much noise today
The noise of technology
The noise that money makes
The noise of promotions
The noise of hype
But most of all the noise
Of terrible excitement
The agitated state of modern life
A frenzy
And the volume is intense

Without a certain quiet
There can be no philosophy
Not religion
Not painting or poetry
Not any kind of worthwhile art

We may lose it all
And the quiet at the center of the soul
That art demands
No pictures can be painted
In the midst of pandemonium

2015 / 2019 / 2020 / 2021 / 2022

PINGS

At a certain age constipation
Is more worrying than cancer
We need to lighten up to fly away

Like great birds
That must test themselves
Against the promise of the universe
To be carried off in the mighty blows
To heights beyond
Those we thought possible

To strange places now unknown
Light years on light years away
Our nature is to soar
Avoiding it is poisonous
Soul murder
In the first degree

Suicide

It's not just the Earth
That flows below us when we fly
History and time make their own landscapes

Ours is the freedom of the new
But we must remember to look back
If we are to learn
To rid ourselves of cluttered heads and hearts
To embrace the anguish of the way it is
To have the courage to accept
Hopelessness

We follow the river of our dreams

Over the many years
With all the change
The Human condition remains
More or less the same
Hungry-hearted
Life long seekers
Of love and approbation

But the skies we fly
Are sometimes strung
With black clouds lachrymose
Lashing us with winter's wicked winds
Hard frozen tears

We must not forget our pasts
But never blame them
For our deformities
Embrace our ideals
For a more Human future

Time transcends

Our planet Earth
A time machine
Our actions
Our decisions
Our responsibilities
But how does one deal
With their anxieties ?
The price we pay for our Humanity

We negotiate a new actuality
Until creation stops
As it is
Actuality
Is an ever changing thing

So long as the Universe
Expands
By the sonar sounds of our inner ears
We listen for the pings

Regard the galaxies
With great respect
Work at being worthy

Our dreams are blueprints
Just as they are mockeries
For the Truth
To be revealed

Sometimes
Painted in our poems

Equilibrium
A high wire act
A study in complexity
We need to find the answers to
Or we will have to settle
For insanity

Yet things seem worse
Than they really are

We sit astride the chaos of the Universe
Like Kubrick had Slim Pickens
Sit astride
A thermonuclear device

Tragedy
Sometimes a sinner's song
That tempts us with its harmonies

2015 / 2018 / 2020 / 2021 / 2022

EVE AND ADAM

You and I were Eve and Adam
The first two
For a while
The only people in the world
And even if we had thought of it
We had nothing
To cover up our nakedness

Though still naked
We are apart
I'm homeless
An animal
In an Iron cage

Who will be the last to remember
All the greatness
That has been created ?
Who will recall the greatness of Man ?
All we have revealed
Between the beginning and now ?

Who will keep the memory
Of how we loved
And all we felt
As we clung to one another
In the time before the end of us ?

Morality is out of date
We sing
But in the chorus
Of others' low ideals

Choking on the bullshit
Rammed down our throats
Our minds controlled
Without our even knowing it

A pandemic of social evils
As contagious as the plague of 1348
Everyone infected
No one left unfouled by it
The home infected too

We behaved like idiots
So pompous with one another
So fucking cruel
Something artificial
Something showy crept in

I think the trouble came
From outside of us
We mistook the lack of spirit in our time
The universal evil
The weight too much
To keep out of our lives

We dragged it in
Like the cold on a winter's day
But we noticed it not
We took no precautions
And it destroyed us
And the beautiful thing we had

We listened to clichés
And all the bad advice
From those who we thought loved us
The Human Ego
Is a powerful
And tricky
And mostly evil thing

And so is Jealousy
For the jealous never wish you well
Though they know it not
We had so much more than most
We became a target

We were smothered by the meanness
Our own trivialities
And for our mistakes
For most of which
I take responsibility

I suffered for all that came upon us
Rather than trying to make it right
I quarreled with history
As if trying to get even

I remember when all we wanted
Was children
And world peace
For all the children to be fed
A time when we would listen to reason
When we heard it
Without regards
From whom it came

The time when it was right and normal
To listen
To all our conscience told us
To do or not to do
When we had respect for one another
And the love we shared

The end can never justify the means
Where people are concerned
The slippery slope to ensure the end of us

There was a sudden jump to blood and tears
But mercy and compassion too

But it was all too fucking late

Focused on our own agendas now
To the exclusion of all else

Now it's Man's insanity
Values so fucked up
Unredeemable
We're more savage
Than we've ever been
Heading to the slaughter

Eventually
We will be expected to pay

But my heart insists
There's still a chance for us
With the love that was ours
And ours only
I believe in that kind of happiness
After all we lived it

I know you were mistaken
When you said you knew my heart
Unless you lied
I would hate to think
You consciously misled me

Now you take
The most unkind view
Of who I was and am
As if you see me
In a distorted mirror
In a Coney Island funhouse

But even if I thought
I could stop loving you
My heart would not allow it

The sinners sing Satan's songs
Felt instead of heard
Perform his scalding symphonies
Dirge like in a minor key
Syphilitic sirens in stiletto heels
Seduce Satan's sons
Spreading lust's poison
Through the underworld.

2015 / 2017 / 2020 / 2021 / 2022

SACRAMENT?

My redemption lies
In the pools of Truth
That fill
The notches of your green
Kentucky Irish Eyes
My forgiveness
Is your natural grace
My happiness
Forever
Your sweet heart

But thinking of that sacred place
Between your legs
Keeps me alive

Foolishness
A necessity
With all the fighting
All the wars
All the petty arguments
All the baseless boasting
All the pitiful courage it takes
To keep knocking the chip
Off God's shoulder

And the timidity
And primal fear
That can turn a tree into a ghost
Or a shadow
That hands my heart
A frightened sorrow

I used to wish
I was a child again
So that I could cry
All the fear away

But I'm old
Been through too much
To be afraid
Of anything
Now

There is a passion for Reality
But very little interest in the way it is

In these times
Reality
Is but another word
For the brutality
We accept all kind of shit
As standard

The people are condemned
And do what they must
To acquire more of everything
They work
They even kill
They humiliate

Baring their teeth like Barbary Apes
And the monkeys who gather excrement
To throw at those who enrage them
Or those who pay to stare at them
In their cages in the zoos

It is good to know the way it is
Even if it's painful

I feel estranged
From everyone and everything
Cut off
Separated

Not so much
By my age
But for my preoccupations
Too different
Too removed
And by my point of view

I lean far to the left
In a right leaning world
Towards the spiritual and the mystical
The metaphysical and magical
Each of which require
A leap of faith
In this show-me world

Few understand
My approach to life
I no longer have a purpose
In the practical world

But live aesthetically
Free
To consume the environment
It's part of the job

I've been absorbed
With the exploration
And the care of my soul
In pain and somewhere bleeding
I do my best to express it all
In paint and words

But I'm finished
Feeling sorry for myself
I accept
It is what it is

No longer will I try
To transfigure my heartbreak
Into observation first
Instead translate experience
Directly into art

Some days I see the sun afire
As if there is no death

The Human Being
Who values himself
(For the right reasons)
Has an obligation
To warn the rest of us
When it gets out of hand

Who made shit a sacrament?

Nature
God
The final Truth
The way it is

Mankind is crazy
Melancholy and morose
But to our credit
Metaphysically aware

The way it is
It is
And will likely be
For a moment
At least

We have found the strength
To go on with life
Anyway
This life the way it is
With all its questions
And its too few answers

From the top of our intellects
To the bottom of our dirty miseries
The questions seem impossible to answer
The answers we offer up

A humble try
Too often inane
But try we will
For try we must
We achieve what we can
We hold no claim on any man
Or his ideas

But there's a poverty of Human Soul today
One can see it
In the faces
One passes on the street
Who can blame them
When the city's rats
Are the size of dogs ?

Many things that go on
Inside the Human Head
Are far beyond Man's comprehension
We live in a human and social sea
But a lot of us can't swim

Ideas bathe our brains

The weight of the world
Is upon us all
And more
For man is in a revolutionary state
Becoming

We are not becoming something new
But something long ago we used to be
More brutal
More savage
More tribal too

There are no secrets
Everything will be revealed

The spirit feels cheated
Even outlawed today
Defiled corrupted and fragmented
Very badly hurt

Yet the Human Soul knows what it knows
And it can not be discarded
Or denied

Its growth
The aim of everything

Mankind can not be anything
But what it is

O we yearn
And we suffer and we mourn
Yet with it all we still go on
And somehow
Some of us make art

The moon is good
For the ills of man
A metaphysical pill
So say the Metaphysicians
The doctors of the human soul

Many think
It's a good idea
To explore the universe

But others think we should
Take care of business first
On Earth
Before we step out
To romance the stars

But I see it as an urgency
For if we wait
We're sure to die
Psychically

Unless
We are annihilated first
By weapons made by man
Or the man caused destruction
Of the environment

Human life in two hundred years ?
Three to five against

2015 / 2020 / 2021 / 2022

CIBORIUM

Man's unconscious
A lawless place
Independent
No rules

How else would it be possible
For humans to create?
Unencumbered
Without limits set

Without edges
We are free
To blow the space away

Some embrace their gifts with gratitude
Some don't give a shit
They spend their time instead
Working their banalities
Studying their defects and deformities
Talking to their shrinks

All of us suffer from
Longing and dejection

The wasting breath
Of humiliation
Blows bleakley on the fallen soul
And the agony
In the paranoia
Thinking
God loves others more than me

When the Human Soul is full of grace
It's radiant
Like the seventeen billion trillion stars
Humble us

Triumph long denied to us
Microscopic to the galaxies

These are evil days
Corpus domini nostri Christi
The ciborium has come to him

2015 / 2019 / 2020 / 2021 / 2022

PRAYER

I have a voice and I will sing
For better or worse
I'll not be silenced
I've made that mistake

Fools
And players by others' rules
Are always safe
Every try involves some risk
There's always a price to pay
For reaching

One begins to see many things
As blindness overtakes him
We hear God's music more
When it's the only thing we hear

The heartless love to profit
From others' misery

We deceive ourselves
From day to day
But Truth wins out
Eventually

Justice is God's alone
To mete out on Earth
As He sees fit

No one wants
To be cast out
Into the night
Which has no end

Punished
For presuming to be born
For all our pride
And for our
Far too many sins

Now and then I wish for death
But know
Calm can be found
In the middle of the maelstrom

The eye of a hurricane
The joining spokes of a wheel
At the hub

God seems to have forsaken me
But there is still much work
For me to do

Lovers hear the ones they love
Before they call
The gifted hear the music
Before it is played
The fleet win the race
Before it's run
Synchronicity
The Morphic Field

Blessed is he who speaks His name
Without words
The deaf
Who can hear a pin drop
In the midst of a tornado
And the blind who see further
Than we will ever see
Blessed are the old
Whose hearts are young
Listen closely to the meek
For they will be our masters

Holy
Are those who feed the children
Though
They've nothing for themselves to eat

But who am I to write a prayer ?
It was I but not me

2015 / 2019 / 2020 / 2021 / 2022

FATHER FRIEND

That summer morning
In the year I came of age
I had a job to do
Before I went to work
Beachcombing

Picking up paper
Left on the beach
By the city folk
Who didn't care

I set out to find my father
And his Runyonesque friends

Once again
He stayed out all night
Never did come home to sleep
My mother alone
In their bed

Survivors of World War Two
When men were men and more
Heroes
Larger than life
They did what they wanted to
When they wanted to do it

It was the weekly floating crap game
That kept pop away
That August night

I found him amongst the hanging meat
Dressed for winter but no gloves
(For he had to feel the dice)
In the walk-in freezer
In the back
Of Hochberg's Kosher Butcher Shop

So filled with smoke
Anyone who ate the meat
Was sure to die of Cancer
I could not see or breathe
My old man rescued me

What say we put the feed bag on ?
Breakfast with my father meant he won
Next time he would lose
And more than likely
Lose a lot

But even then
I somehow knew
One need not cross a bridge
Unless
It's the one in front of you

I was glad
For his good mood that day
So I did not give him shit for staying out
Like my mother told me to

I was his pride and joy
And from time to time he would let me know
In his macho- man war- vet way
Pop was not what one would call objective
He might well have been
The king of subjectivity

Every day I thank the Lord
He did not live to see
What has become of me
It would have killed him if he did

But it's always
Death the victor
In the end
I suffer still
His loss
Fifty years and more
Ago

Guilty of not doing more
Guilty of thinking that
The day he died may have been
The best day of my life
A kind of liberation
And the very worst of course
My old man was dead

Fathers and sons
Complications

Somewhere it is eight bells
On the open sea
The moonless midnight pitch
A strange kind of purple haze
Keeps the stars from view
The darkness is inscrutable

The noisy silence
Sounds like the dirt
Hitting my father's coffin
As I fill the dead man's grave with it
And the river of my foolish tears
I have never stopped crying

2015 / 2019 / 2020 / 2021 / 2022

THE GREAT DEFLATION

Reason has been nullified
Good sense annulled
Non-stop information
Has taken their place

A nice person is a rarity
(one hardly hears
The word nice anymore)

There is little vigorish
Being kind today
A master plan for love
Is wanting
Angels can't get around as fast
As feelings change

Love has been revolutionized
The old ways replaced
A sexy game
An erotic dance
For those
Who want to get out
On the floor

More primitive
Than it used to be
Like children in a bakery
Give me !
Give me !
Give me !

The intellect without the soul
Has been turned loose
Like long ago the penis was
And now the vagina too

Making love and fucking
Are different things

The sacredness of love debunked
Disowned and discredited
We used to make promises
To those we love

And we tried hard to keep them
There's been a great deflation
Love was once more valuable
Than gold

But the business of sex has never been better
The clothes and cosmetics
The birth control
The fuck-me boots and shoes
Viagra and Cialis
(The fucking fountain of youth)

The psychiatry
The money spent
To soothe the wounds
Patch up deflated egos
The Irony

Anything but love itself
Those who once could love
Have become too unstable to
And then there are the lies

The propaganda of love
The movies and T.V.
But real people are not up to
All they hear and see

They should know it's fiction
They should know it's a fairy tale
Few depict the way it is
When two people are in love
Instead they act the way
They think love was meant to be

The act of love
The lovers then
The actors in
What has become
A tragedy

Best to keep it simple

People old enough
Come to understand
The prophet Job too well
By a certain age
One has become
Experienced in suffering

Of all animals
We are the only one
Born ignorant
Forced to learn
Almost everything we will ever know
Or need to

God is present
In the process of all things
All of us becoming
For becoming is all there is

Until at least
The end of the Universe expanding
At many times the speed of light
And then we hit the wall of death
The Universe the wall of Actuality

While we can
The thing to do is learn
We will be truly free
But
More time will be needed
Something we will have to earn

It's hard to know today
What makes sense
And what is foolishness
When we should laugh
When we should cry

Christ died on the cross
Laughed at
And scorned
Bleeding
From the wound in his side
Sanctifying the Earth
With His sacred blood

And the hounds in Caesar's clothes
Bayed the kill

His power and His glory
Locked
Into the weakness of a man
Accepting His human limitations
His sacrificial Humanhood
Nothing much has changed

He saved all men
By dying like a man dies
The most magnificent of men
They nailed Him to the cross
To make Him suffer
They drove spikes into
His holy hands and feet

But He moved beyond the pain
To some kind of Godly ecstasy
And the doubting
Perhaps His greatest gift

Human Beings have many flaws
That must be understood
For these flaws
Are the essence
Of our humanity

There are countless things
That make a man a man
The oldest questions in the world
Why and what and who am I ?

Doubt and ambiguity
The price
We pay for the ride

2015 / 2020 / 2021 / 2022

AWFULLY CLOSE

Her wild beauty a veil
To the strange thing in her heart
When she looked into my eyes
She was exploring my soul
Mystical and beautiful
Beyond all dreams
And all imaginings

We lived and loved
Together for years
Gladness gilded our days

Why must Man
Sow corruption in his soul
That always leads to woe?

No mortal Man
Save Jesus Christ
Was ever perfect
But she was awfully close
Day by day
She weaved her magic spell around me
I came to know her hidden being
She grew more lively
And more strange

Paradise
Had overtaken the Earth
An Angel
Her halo and her mysteries

But our joy was not near long enough
Storms follow bright dawnings

There are other factors
In the world at play
Than the love
Of a woman and a man
For one another

Long memories of short lived scenes
Thoughts of joyous hours

Why is it
We do not pause
To appreciate those times of joy
While they are happening?

Happiness
Seldom seems so
But for when looked back upon
From times of woe

Like the beauty of a landscape
One must leave
To fully know
It's hard to tell
The forest from the trees

One winter's day
She told me it was over
Eventually she went away

Beside myself with sadness
I was in great pain

With the years the suffering
That keened hurt
Became a deep vibration inside me
A bruised soul
A remembering

Though bowed down
With sadness still
There are thoughts
That glitter in my heart

I share this common woe
Of grief and loss
As I attempt to find my way
Through the chaos
And the pain

Some mourners load the air with lunacies
Their Human needs are stuck
In the depths of their souls
Their tears fall fast

But who can know another's heart?
Who can get at his own
To mend it when it's broken?

In that time between
The tic and toc
The then and now
I've grown old
And beaten down
And mortified

I stand astride the grave
Nothing but love
To offer now
Not to her
Not to my kids
Not to anyone

To me she is forever young
Always very beautiful
Her alabaster skin
Her Irish green
Kentucky notched eyes

The perfect lover
The best of friends

In the end
She chose to believe
The world in which
She felt forced to live
Instead of having faith in me
She dared not take the risk

And now
She will barely talk to me
It hurts
More than I can tolerate

My instinct
Is to turn the pain to anger
But who is there to turn it to?
Myself?

I never thought I'd feel this
Resignation I mean
I tell myself
To know the truth
Is worth the fucking pain
Self- deception
Is a children's game

2016 / 2018 / 2020 / 2021 / 2022

AFFIRMATIONS

Those who think of me as misanthropic
Do me great wrong
Though there are reasons
That could make them feel way
But my heart and soul
Are filled with love
Like they've always been

I've been often wounded
But with everything
I feel the same
About this at least
As I always did

But I tried too hard
Bit off more than I could chew
Fiery
I'm a person of some passion

Perhaps I've been misunderstood

I took on things
I had no reason to believe
I could achieve

I am left to wonder why?
To ask myself
Who the fuck I thought I was?
Was it all some kind of grand delusion?

I prefer to think
Those things I've tried and will
Come from my heart
This heart
Overflowing with love

The respect I sought
Was never for myself
But for the work I did
The art

And money
But another tool
For better doing it

It was never about the approbation
I never did want or need
The work I chose
Or chose me
Was not the kind of work
To lead to frivolity

The happiness I did achieve
Was of another kind entirely
You and the kids of course
And the kind which comes with knowing
I've done the best I could

With it all
I think
Mine has been a life well lived

But banished now
Stripped of everything
A future that for me
I could live with or without
There are worse things in life than death

I pray for some joy
But it's been sometime
Since I've been happy
I've suffered years of anguish here
Tormented and alone

Perhaps the pain
Was meant
To stoke the fires
That once burned in me

I write my epitaph
He lived and loved
He tried everything
He achieved those things he could

My effort was to make affirmations
To make work that was beautiful
To find God's light
And to show it to the world
But most of all
Was made by someone
Who wanted to ease the pain a little
That so many people feel

To keep aware
Of the transcendental
Beauty
Brotherhood and love

And art which affirms all things
Without which there would be
No counterpoint
To the terror in the world
Nothing to set against the horrors
Man continues to inflict on himself

2016 / 2017 / 2020 / 2021 / 2022

TANTRUM

He sees the rainbow's top
The apex of the valley
Between the Irish hills
I mean he sees it
Like it's under a microscope
And it haunts him with its beauty
He can hardly stand to look

A mysterious significance
A dream
Truth perhaps
Obscured by color
And the sun

There he is
Hanging on the cross
Clinging hard to life
It will turn out like this
For all of us

Even Jesus had a role to play
But his was on
A grander Godly stage
The body of a man never wants to die
No matter the condition of the soul inside

A close up of a suicide
An acting out
The face of lost hope
The tantrum of a child

2016 / 2020 / 2021 / 2022

A BIGGER THING

In youth
We are
In old age
We seem to be
The smile is the vehicle
Of all Man's ambiguities
We often smile
When we deceive
Or when hatching some petty plot

But it's dark in woe
And I am swimming in a sea of it

It may be the sacred promise
And deepened by the wise
The inestimable compensation
For the worst of woe

To purge
The mistakes of man
To replace it with a shadowed Truth
The silk purse made of the sow's ear
The fucking silver lining

The darkness splits itself
Into forked flames of light and fire
At last
We see things as they are

Yet the shadows will
Again descend
False outlines
Once more revealed
But now unable to deceive

For the presence of their falsest aspects
Return impressions of the fired ones
Once phosphorescent
But again
Concealed

Like lightning
Only grief will clarify

But Man is weak
Weak enough to choose
The false joy of illusion
Rather than to suffer the Truth

I am nothing
And I know it
It is all a dream I've dreamed
I dreamed I dreamed
But there is no sin in dreaming

Dead
We dream not
For us
The rising sun
Will rise no more

Lord lay me down
Below the Earth's soft sod
Beneath the tester of the infinite
Like emperors and kings before me

I will sleep
Death's dark sleep
Death
The great democracy
One grows to love the idea of it

Some heads are crowned by gold
Others crowned with thorns
But
The dead are all the same
Worm food and dust

Fate has made a maniac of me
Things swim before my eyes
That make me wild
And when I think of all the ambiguities
Which together seem a unity
Like the razor wire fences here
I can not overleap

Last lingerings of happiness
Licked up on me
Like flames of fire

I stand astride a bottomless abyss

I teeter
At the edge of oblivion
Desperate
Nothing to lose
I'm free
To do anything

No consequence
Can hurt me now
I'm a dangerous man
Beware

There are many things
Unsuspected from without
That are as yet
Undivulgible

The very dangers
That stab at me
A mystery

With the soul of an artist
Who wants to think
I make my work
For a bigger thing

Though I feel death and woe within
I paint a piece of happiness
Against my broken heart
And bursting head
Against this dismal lassitude
And damned lacrimony
This inability to sleep
Against this whirling
And this craziness

I still bear up
I give blow for blow
A dangerous old man

Fuck with me
And you'll get hurt
Those animals who heap me so
Like the White Whale Ahab

The more art I make
The deeper I dive inside myself
I sometimes see
The elusiveness
Of the Truth I seek
That I'm ready to die for

I feel gifted by loftiness
Compelled to watch
As it is brought down
By the money-men
And their sycophants

There's a freedom
In committing
To stand
Against all odds
For one's beliefs
A certain freedom
In that kind of surrender

2016 / 2018 / 2020 / 2021 / 2022

A CERTAIN SATISFACTION

There are many ways
To most destinations
But in the end
All roads lead to death

The money men talk of change
Their grand designs
Are just new forms
Of the same fucking miseries

We witness shocking things
That change the paradigms
Oppress us
With hideous new emotions
An incubus upon our hearts
A shadow on our brains

With time we learn
To breathe again
With an even greater freedom
A new elasticity
In the way we use our minds

But then alas
The lamentation
The worm will turn
The winds of change will bring the pain
We have experienced before
Once again to drown
In tears of disenchantment

Nothing hurts a person more
Than the death of a dream
There is little dreaming here
This place
Where dreams go to die

Most of us have very little
Of importance to say
It's mostly noise
In the failed attempt
To prove
We are human
We try to justify

To show the Gods who put us here
That we are worth the space on Earth
We seem to think the noise we make
Will make us feel less lonely

Everything is evanescent
Even the pain

Take heart !
For in living life
You have won
A great and moral victory
Paid for by so many defeats

In surviving all the sorrows
A certain satisfaction may be gained

I will not paint a frenzied man
Nor sing of lost hope
Those things that once inspired us
Now bring us to despair

Let us leave it up to fate
Days unfold the way they will
All we can do
Is react to them

Believe enough to pray

Let us stretch our hands toward Heaven
Face the threatening skies
Tremble
Cry

If we must
Look
For the penetrating light
To mark the end
And guide us home

Or we can wait
For the fire to surround us

2016 / 2017 / 2020 / 2021 / 2022

BLOOD AND TEARS

With His faith
We too could walk on water
Move mountains to the sea
Bring courage to the weak
Make the blind man see
Raise our loved ones from the dead
Expel the demons
From those who seek
Sincerely
Bring the lame to their feet
Clean away the Leprosy

We are dying
To be reborn again
The glory of the resurrection
And the light
To be reunited with the Father

On the other hand
This leery-lover
This joker
This charlatan
This magician
Who can make us think
We are in Heaven
When we are
Most definitely in Hell

This collector of Human Souls
This culprit
This criminal
This motherfucking thief
This stealer of hearts
The Lord of the Kingdom of Despair
This fallen angel
This antiChrist
This great destroyer

Nothing has been refused him
But faith and prayer
Soothing and consoling love
That is not of this world
Obeyed
His word in certain situations law

Suppose Satan
Made a bid for your soul
Would you exchange it for the power of a God?
Would you exchange it for a pot of gold?

If you could hear the music
The angels make for God alone
Music
That moves the soul to ecstasy
Would you be willing to pay the price
For eternity?

The killing toil is ended
The unceasing physicality
The peasant and the laborer
With their blood and tears
Have won the right
To think of themselves
As people

For the first time in history
Their souls are blessed with liberty
But the price paid was terrible
In grief and blood and misery
Freedom takes some getting used to
And so far
It's not been
Altogether a success

We have fallen
Into an ugly world
A good portion of the people
Are now clinically depressed
The world it seems needs Prozac
More than gasoline

One percent of the people now
Are locked away
In jails like this
Home to those who broke the laws
Written by the vassals of the money-men
To keep the money in the hands
Of those of whom
Already have
So much of it

We think we are original
But there is nothing new in the world
Yet every soul is unique
Though captive of the Human form
So hateful
So grotesque
So many body holes
That smell like shit

Covered with cosmetics
Calmed by drugs
Dominated by our genitalia

It's as if at birth
We were all issued
A ticket through Hell
Living life is like a trip
Through a Coney Island sideshow

Monstrosities surround us
We offend God
With our obscenities
How terrified our souls must be!

With all this vehemence
With all this suffocating passion

I'm aware of my negativity
As it regards my views of life
For many years of mine
I've lived at the extreme

One cannot come out intact
From a place like this
I am harder than I've ever been
I brutally simplify

One needs a certain swagger here
In order to survive

There have been times
Over the past few years
I've wondered
If I'm still alive

Or if all of this has been delusion
Some kind of a demented dream
A glimpse of Hell perhaps
A surreal hallucination
A bad fucking mushroom trip

Am I an actor in a science fiction play ?
The quintessential horror show
The projections of a man
Made mad by life
Made crazy in living it

The way it played out
Wild and sorry
Too often sad
But worst of all
Almost all the time
Terrified

2016 / 2018 / 2020 / 2021 / 2022

CHANGING STATES

The big bang ongoing
The universe still expands
While out from the center
This rock we ride

The emptiness of space
The long dark amnesia

In the end to change
But holding tight
To an endless vitality
In our prayers
We never die

What's left of me is breaking up
Chunks of me are melting
Sparkling with pain
Floating off

Stripped
Of one more person
Dear to me
One more reason to go on

Forever gone
Taken
Set aside
Past away

I can't get used to it
Anyway I won't

There are it's true
Too many people in the world
And there are worse things than death
That can happen to a Man

But only the good die young
Think about what that means
About the rest of us
Those of us who survive to old age

Our too small supply of humanity
We exist on fumes of grace
Soon to be Human no more

Some still try to transcend
Being Human I mean
But some believe transcendence
Is kin to disorder

Methinks transcending
Is a good idea
But it's not up to us
We don't get to decide
Things of that magnitude
(If we decide anything at all)
His will be done
And we all know it

Cheated and outraged
Corrupted and defiled
And very badly hurt
Our souls lost
In the mayhem

Things once known
Will be known again
Time is a circle
The Universe turns 'round

The growth of the spirit
The main reason to exist
Perhaps the only one
We are who we are
Creatures on the verge of oblivion

When it comes
We will have nothing to say
For like it or not
Death is an angel of God

I am full of strong impressions
Of eternity
Must be my age
Or the mood I'm in
Or both

We most want
Another state of being
A defused state of consciousness
It's Truth we want
Experience
Not comprehension

I know too much
Of the Human Heart
To be untouched
By the disquietude of others
It is hard to be happy
When other people hurt
And someone is always hurting

Pain comes with creation
And as the universe is still expanding
Creation is ongoing
Thus
The ubiquity of pain
The ever present agony of birth

There is a wisdom that is woe
And a woe that is wisdom
And there is Truth
Those who seek the Truth are higher
Than someone stuffed with facts
Gathered on the fucking internet

We see the ambiguities
All mystery
A double edged sword
Out of which parables
Of thinking phantoms rise
Tidings of infinite gloom

And all the mystical moonlights spent
Pondering
The constant state of change

I float into great visions
Metaphysical imaginings
Long and for forever gone
Finally

2016 / 2018 / 2019 / 2020 / 2021 / 2022

SERIAL SINNER

What good is this half-death
Without oblivion?
This being set aside
This sitting in the bleachers
Forced to watch your life go on
Without you in it

To be forced to know
Your children live
A life
Without their father there
To imagine their laughter
And their tears
Unable to comfort them
Unable to smell their sweaty hair
At the end of their play
Unable to keep them safe
At the end of the day

Forced to think
Of your own true love
In the arms of another
Saying the same breathless things
Once said only to you
Impotent
Unable to act
As if you were already fully dead

Happy to know
Their life goes on without you
But tough to take when half- alive
A silent movie on a screen
A dining room
With one empty seat
The one you used to sit in

One presumes in death
Profound peace
At least
The still of non-being

This is the in-between
The neither here nor there
The worst of everything

Consigned to live for years
In an iron cage
Stuck in Limbo
The quintessential metaphysical
Clusterfuck

Like being in a master's kitchen
Without the sense of taste or smell
Stuck
With Mozart and an instrument
Without the ability to hear
Invited to watch Rembrandt paint
Unable to see

Give me life or death
One or the other
Anything is better than this

There is nothing one can do on Earth
That has not been done
And it is only in different deaths
That man can go
Where he has never been before

It's getting old
My brain has atrophied
A serial sinner
I've sinned my share
I long for death
Free of guilt

Perhaps when God forgives me
I'll reclaim the faith
I had in younger years
To pray again
To hit my knees
To confess
To make amends
To live to say I'm sorry
To those of whom I hurt

I scream
At the same time laugh
Sure of myself again
The mania of a maniac
I've put an end to doubt

It is better to soar in dreams
That can not be realized
Than to wallow
In the muck and mire
Of what they think of as Reality

2016 / 2019 / 2020 / 2021 / 2022

QUARANTINE

They're making plans
To colonize
The planet Mars
Man's first big move in years
Into the universe

Another chance to fuck it up

Exploration is fine with me
It can't be stopped anyway
But we must think twice
Before we spread
The disease that's Man
Across the Universe

First find the cures
For all that ails us
Before we step into the galaxies
Make sure we know which ones
Are galactically contagious
Quarantine all of us
Until we're sure we're clean

Find the sense
Govern our hubris
Seek advice
From the other forms of life
We may encounter
In this stepping out

Holier than thou
We put our so called sinners
In metal cages
And leave them there for years
For the greater good
They say

A continent of psychopaths
A planet full of vicious fucks
Most of those who give it thought
Hate themselves
Or should

Helpless
In constant need of explanation
The healthiest one
Among us all
A neurotic fuck
More afraid of seeming stupid
Than we are of death

Is this what we are planning
To impose upon the Universe?
What makes us think
The Martians will allow it?

Duty is a hateful thing
A misery
And painful
But necessity
A creative force

In the end
With all our plans
We will obey the will of God
For it will turn out
The way He wants it to
Anyway

If He wants to doom the Universe
Man no doubt
Will have a part to play
For no creatures
In the history of the galaxies
Destroy as well as we

So many things touched by man
Have turned to shit
Like the Earth's environment
Destroyed in record time
Galactically

The Big Bang occurred
Almost fourteen billion years ago
Man has only been around
A couple of hundred thousand years

Man is loony
Histrionic and eccentric
Sanity
Here on Earth
Is insanity
To the rest of the Universe

It may well be that soon
We will be forced to find
A new planet
On which to live
Which orbits another Sun

If it's True
Ours will burn out
In about six billion years
We're closer
To the end of life on Earth
Than we are to The Big Bang
The beginning of the end
The end of the beginning

We spend our years
Trying to escape
We lose ourselves
In imagination and dreams
In trips to Disneyland
Watching M.T.V.
Spending time in the virtual
Virtual reality
Violent video games
Drinking
Smoking weed
Anything
That for the moment
Takes the pain away

Anything but this

2016 / 2018 / 2020 / 2021 / 2022

ONCE A DAY

Once a day
For about a minute
I felt like I once did
For hours or more
Whole days would pass
When I would soar
In touch with God
The Creative Force

Once a day
I knew what I was missing
Once a day
I would wonder why
I was still alive

Once a day
The light broke through
Which made it clear
How very dark it was in here

Once a day
I could laugh
But I've not since found
Anything to laugh about

Once a day
Like I do right now
I feel I can sing

Once a day
Is not enough
But it's a hell of a lot better
Than never

Once a day
If only for a moment
I believe
I can still love

Once a day
I feel the need to create
Which only makes waiting for
That once a day worse

Once a day I feel like living
The rest of the time
I yearn for death

All day
I wait
For that once a day

2016 / 2020 / 2021 / 2022

EASIER SAID THAN DONE

I've grown conscious
Of the neglect
Written on the faces I confront
A wake up call
A message

Only a fool
At my old age
Would bite off more
Than he can chew
I should know myself by now
But so few ever do

Many things
Are easier said
Than done

I used to see your love for me
Shining
In your notched Irish eyes
Nothing needed to be said
You knew
And so did I

But now your eyes
Once so warm with love
Have turned to ice
Frozen out
I freeze to death

A man's own lips
Entrap him
Brought to pain
By his own words
Shit storms and clusterfucks
Self-projected

Stealing souls
The business of fallen angels
And business has never been better

They discovered
If the price is right
Many are happy
To sell their souls away

Money
Has never been a problem
For Satan and his minions
They are happy to pay

We must discern
Between bad and good
Ignorance
Yields discontent
Unrighteousness
Gives birth to lies

The black-hearted are destroyed
An eternity in Hell

We are torn between
The world to which we aspire
And the one in which we're forced to live
The source
Of our unrest
And much of our pathology

I see no one
Save the saints in stained glass windows
In the paintings by the masters made
The gargoyles carved in stone
Come to life
To confront me
I am stuck in here for now
But for my books

But the gates will one day open
I will walk amongst the living
Once again
The truly alive
I will see the light
Stand beneath the moon and stars
Free !
Fucking free !

2016 / 2018 / 2019 / 2020 / 2021 / 2022

THE CITY

Open lots
Condemned burned out buildings
Addicted dancers contemplate
The soles
Of their last pair of dancing shoes
Blown away
Wrecked and ruined
And slowly dying

Storefront churches
Mountains of trash
Mostly women now
Their men in jail
Holy homeless people

Cops shoot anything that moves
Especially
If the thing that moves
Is brown or black

Humans piled one on another
In piles of bricks that scrape the sky
One must train himself
To be brave enough
Not to be terrified

For the smell of death is in the air
Crazy people left to rot
All around things disintegrate
The streets
And the people on them
Continue to be mean

Hearts are hard
Heartbreak and hunger
Victims of Reality
Are everywhere

Even those
Who in their mansions sit
On the sidestreets
Off Park Avenue
But the hunger there
Is of a different sort
Theirs is pathological

2016 / 2020 / 2021

WELL REHEARSED

The cacophony
A wall of sound
No one can hear above
The crowd
Sweats through the summer night
Sweltering
The carnival near the beach

Off the boardwalk
Near the empty concrete tower
Used
In our fathers' war
To watch for Nazi submarines

Everyone is hot as Hell
But those descending
Shrieking as the coaster dives
Twisting and plunging down
Lives hung on centrifugal force
For a brief time weightless

The calliope's music
The barkers yell and scream
Coaxing suckers to the sideshows
The Bearded Lady
The Cyclops
Sword Swallowers and the Strong Man
Milo the Mule-Headed Boy

Pitchmen sell above the crowd
Hawking their wares
Explosions light the sky
Colored lights cascading
Fizzling
In the darkened sea
Bursts of fire blinding

An undercurrent of hostility
The press of sexuality
Everything is for sale
The city girls on the make
A ship of fools
A great fucking show

An atheist on a soapbox
Rails against the existence of God
Nonetheless God there is
An inscrutable divineness in the world
Positively present everywhere
Ubiquitous
Here in this room
The force that moves my brush and pen

I am content
As He made me
In my humanity
With all my faults
With all that's base about me
My soul remains immaculate
Without a shadow
Pure as the whitest marble
Constant as the Northern Star

But now I know not how to think
And I have forgotten how to dream
Yet
I yearn for Truth
And I still know how to pray

Henceforth
Ours will be a wordless wooing
Until we meet again
I was the cause of your suffering
Yet you overcame
And I rejoice in your overcoming
It makes me love you more

Rehearsing the part of Death
We learn how to better live
My six years in here
Have been an education
I've earned my Ph.D
Midstate
My Harvard and my Yale

I know well my cues
And I know my part by heart
I'll be ready when the curtain rises
Ready for the rest of the show
To leave all that remains of me
In the final act
Then watch the curtain fall

The greater the artist
Is in his work
The slimmer the chances
He will earn his bread from it
So much for Reality

There are certain things
In the soul of Man
That can not be sung or painted
Which doesn't mean we shouldn't try
To sing and paint them

2016 / 2017 / 2020 / 2021 / 2022

TEARS OF BLOOD

I fail to see the Vigorish
In his trip to Pakistan
It may well turn out to be
A great experience
A great opportunity to learn
But meaningless
If he returns from this vacation
Maimed
Or in a body bag

I'm worried so for him
The risks too high
For the potential rewards

Sometimes it's true
If nothing is ventured
Nothing will be gained
And sometimes it's true
When nothing is ventured
There is something gained
If only in retaining
That which you might have lost

Why travel half-way around the world
To walk out on a shaky limb
When there are forests full right here?
Elias be careful
You mean the world to me

But I am locked away in here
And over there
You will be on your own
Knocking on the gates of Hell
In the middle of the maelstrom
The vortex of mayhem
The center of human madness today

The people wear vests of bombs
The drones strike
Surgically

American Sniper
A hundred kills and more
Mass murderers
Are dealt with as heroes here
Each bullet shot paid for
In someone else's pain

Death rains down on Human Beings
In tears of blood
Another sixty blown apart
In the name of some God
So much for thou shalt not kill
So much for the high standards of democracy

The Patriot Act and waterboards
It's all about the money men
In their lust for more money
More power and control
More oil

But we are culpable
For allowing them
To perpetrate this shit

Three hundred twenty million suckers

Warships and aeroplanes
Flying fucking fortresses
Bunker busters
Bombs with high I.Q.s
All kinds of guns and hand grenades
A million I.E.D.s
Children blown to pieces
Once again the world has been
Brought to its knees

We're talking big business here
The worship of the almighty buck
Big profits made by building things
Purposed to destroy and kill
And fortunes paid to these same men
To build back again
That which
They were paid a fortune to destroy

Their imaginations prodigious
But evil

They tell us
That a man
Has a right to earn his bread to live
No matter how many mothers mourn
To sate
The rich man's appetites

They do it in the name of God
Inventing and selling
Using these instruments
Of murder and slaughter

Money money money money
Give me more the rich men say
Naked we came to this world
And naked we will be taken away
And anyway
Currency is worthless in Heaven
Where love
Is the coin of the realm

It's come to be that God
Is just a word
Now evil mostly triumphs
Virtue is destroyed

But we must still try
We must stand up
We dare not surrender

An example for the future ones
Who in their turn
Will stand for Truth
And with God's help
May be strong enough
To impose it on the wicked ones

2016 / 2019 / 2020 / 2021 / 2022

BEFORE THE SLAUGHTER

Last stop Auschwitz
The end of the line
The cattle cars
The open doors
Rank
With the smell of excrement
The smell of death

The Jews step off
What's left of them
They know but don't believe
Or they can't or won't
So they do what they are told
(As we Jews are want to do)
Jesus was not
The only Jewish Lamb

Like sheep to the slaughter
They stand for selection
The lucky ones
(It seems to them)
Picked for work
The labor camp
They have more time
An eternity

Like Dostoevsky on the way
To his mock execution

Until they starve to death
Or beaten there
Or killed some other way

The rest piled into waiting trucks
To take them to the showers
They so badly want and need
Relieved of their luggage
By the death camp concierge
They will find it
At the side
Of their brand new beds

But they will sleep
Before they lie in them
And they will sleep forever

They believe
To the end of it
The humanity of credulity
The cruelty of humanity
No one wants to believe
They are about to die

The sign points the way
To disinfection
Another to the undressing hut
They tell them to remember
The number of the rack
They hang their clothes upon
So that they can find them again
After the shower

A German joke
A method of control
Set the illusion
All is well
Any thought of death ridiculous

SS men in white coats
A table full
Towels and soap
The strong smell of disinfectant
Like a locker room at some bizarre
Health club in Hell

The sonderkommandos are out in force
Those Jews who sold their souls to live
A few hours more
They run to help their fellow Jews
Mothers and their kids
Speaking words of some near future
They know will never come
To those they are talking to

They tell them of the camp
As if they would soon see it
The quality of the food
That does not exist
The mail service
The visiting rules

They make it sound like some kind of spa
Or fancy summer camp
When they know damned well
It's Hell

To fool those with minutes to live
To make it all go easily
Evidence of many things
But never banality

A hoax
Maintained until the end
For the good of everyone

To those Germans
The Jew is an enigma
Another reason to hate
(The affirmation of one's failed self through the pain of others)

The Blood Libel
They are all too willing to believe
The Protocols of the Elders of Zion

The undressing hut
Part of the charade
The naked females
Run the gauntlet first
Between the SS men who line the way
To the so-called showers

The Nazis appraise them
At a time like this
Wondering
What they would be like to fuck

Here now the males
The overweight and scrawny ones
Cripples and gray haired
The bald
Their sorry circumcised penises
Shrunk by fright

The closer to death
The harder to fool

Where was God
When all this was happening?

Now locked into the chambers of death
The mournful wails
The resigned prayers
Some die faster than others

The sonderkommandos
Go to work again
They pile the dead on carts
To the mass graves
They were forced to dig

But before they bury them
They search
The mouths of the dead
Hitler wants
The gold in their teeth
Efficiency
A German thing
And greed is universal

Later the crematoriums
In place of common graves
They threw them into ovens
To burn every trace away

The depths of their evil genius
They want the Jewish culture
To completely disappear
No bones to be found
Nobody to blame
No harm no fucking foul

The terrible things
Human Beings
Can bring themselves to do
To win a few more minutes of life
Even if the time is spent suffering

But the gassed are the lucky ones
For in death there is no pain
And with the Human body shed
The soul is set free
To fly away

But it's wrong
To pass judgment on those corrupted
Unless you're God or His Son
Unless you've spent some time
In that person's shoes
The best and worst in anyone
Is the best and worst in everyone
Capable of the greatest good
And the most terrible evil

The mother holds her daughter's hand
Jammed into the showers
The lights go out
The heavy doors slam shut
The screeching iron bolts
Turn
Tighten into place

The wailing!
The Gas!
God have mercy!
They are killing us!

The gas chokes
The disinfectant smell
But much stronger than before
She believes she can see the gas
Pouring through the vent
Near the central column
Opposite
The now locked door

For the last time
She looks upon her daughter
Take me Hashem
Save my little girl

But God must be busy
In some other place

The gas burns and stabs her lungs

Ema (Mother) Ema
The daughter weakly cries

O those bastards !
Those motherfucking maniacs !

The killing camps
The howling
Chaos
The terror in the dark
Shema Yisroel
Even then
The Jew
Will not give up on God

She falls upon her lifeless daughter
Naked bodies fall on her
Her daughter at the bottom
Of the pile
Of the dying
And the dead

She can no longer breathe
Suffocation
A very painful death
Beneath the weight of her fellow Jews
Gas can take as much
As a half hour to kill

But Americans
Should never act
Holier than thou
For we fire-bombed Tokyo
In that same war
The fiery gel sticking
To anyone it touched
Like Napalm in Vietnam

One hundred twenty thousand human beings
Burned to death
Women and children
The old and sick

Burnt to a crisp
In the name of freedom
The most people killed
At one place and time by Man
In Human history

And Dresden too
Europe's jewel
Another hundred thousand burned away
And then we dropped the big one twice

Fifty million humans killed
In World War II
And it seems
We've learned nothing from the sacrifice

Face it !
We are savages
Inventing new
More efficient ways
To kill
Instead of finding
How to fix the Earth
We have so misused
As we must
To survive this century

But it may well be better if we don't
And safer for the Universe
Better if we become extinct
Before we spread
The disease called Man

No more Man
No more want
No more fucking insanity
No more killing based on hate
No more fucking cruelty
No more murder on a galactic scale
No more slaughter of the innocent
No more Human noise
To pollute the galaxies

Never more
To make war
On the Universe
Never more disturb
The way it is
Everywhere but here

But Where was God ?
Where was God
When the meek cried out for him ?
Before the slaughter

2016 / 2018 / 2020 / 2021 / 2022

SAINT VITUS' DANCERS

I love God
But I understand Him not
I bend my knee to no mortal man
I am small
In the sight of God
For He is the God of all of us

He has more than me
To think about
But I am no less
Than what it is I am
One of His children
Omnificent

I wonder
And I hope and love
I weep
But I am not afraid
What more can Man do to me?

But only God
Can know the Human Heart
Each one filled
A thousand souls

And though satellites revolve around me
I revolve around one central Truth
Light
Forever fixed
Luminous

A man is not a coward
Who finds no foe to fight
Anyway
Our toughest fights rage within
Our bruised souls

The world refused me nothing then
But for enough faith and prayer
I thought I had it all
But all I had were things
That do not matter much
Save love
And all those I've lost
Along the way

I never could have peace of mind
I was built of shaky stuff
Most of it
Never wanted arguing
My soul was shook
My woe would have overwhelmed
The strongest one of us

But there was a power of vitality
Within me
In proportion to the sensations
That assailed me
A longing
Nothing could satisfy

To transverse the vastness
To other spheres
An intuitive perception
A cleaning up
A helpless knowledge
A déjà vu
My soul has dried up

I've hungered after things
I didn't want or need
My body writing checks
My soul could never cash

I knew next to nothing
But that little bit of knowledge
May well have saved my ass

On the other hand it may be
The cause of all my troubles
Perhaps
I would have been better off
Without it

Man
A simple creature at heart
A penny's worth of spirit
A quarter's worth of flesh
Joined together
Manifested
Firm
Atom to atom

Seamless yet divided too
Two or three or more in one
Split yet indivisible
An open book
A mystery

Saint Vitus' dancers raise not
The dead from their graves

Men do die and will
If not soon
A few years later
Meaningless galactically

And the world goes on
The way it always did
Dogs still bite
Babies bawl
In the middle of the night
Asses bray
The way they did before the flood
Men fight and reconcile
Only to fight again

We feast
And then we starve
We laugh then weep
We pray and curse
We cheat
Defraud and trick
We beg and lie
We borrow
And we steal

But when the stars are aligned
And the smell is right
We love

And we make it

2016 / 2017 / 2020 / 2021 / 2022

SHARDS

I roar
But no one hears me
I howl
Yet I am less wolf than worm
I bray
An ass
Forsaken
Unlikely to be saved

The Money-Men despise me
Those who sell their lies
To those
Who buy them
In wholesale lots

Twenty first century alchemists
They turn this bullshit
Into a fool's-Truth
Then sell it
But like most of their Reality
It's alternate or virtual

My bones
Are out of joint
My heart
Hot melted wax
Better
To never have been born
Than this

O save me from the Lion's mouth !
Surround me with Unicorns
Keep me alive
To sing to you

Songs of love and gratitude
Songs of remorse
There is only silence
In the pit

More flock to the Valley of Death
Than will ever visit Disneyland

Gather not my soul with sinners
Keep me from the cruel and bloody man
From false witness borne against me

Evil men breathe cruelty
Like dragons fire

Forgotten
Like a man long dead
Broken
I've saved the shards
But I am far from sure
I can be made whole again

Let lying lips be silenced
Those who speak
Against the righteous ones
Lead the meek
To their inheritance

When you speak
Your will is done

The world will ever plot
Against the just
But God stands with them

I'm old
And I've never seen the truly good
Forsaken
I don't expect I ever will

Immortality
From fathers to sons we multiply
Corpses ourselves
Each child a resurrection

The road to Heaven passes through
The center of Hell
Torn against the winds of woe
At white hot heat we burn ourselves
We count our scars
Like we try
To count the stars

O poet
Howl and rage against the pain
Everything is as it is
Nothing much is ever changed
Even with the constant changing

2016 / 2019 / 2020 / 2021 / 2022

BLIGHTED HOPES

In the cold gray light
The clouds repeat
Dangerous
Dangerous

The ocean sings
Die today or die tomorrow
All of us will pass away

I muse on my future
I doubt everything
I bemoan my blighted hopes
And unanswered prayers
Bothered
Beyond the limits of tolerance
Driven mad

I turn again to prayer
No harm in trying
Looking for God's mercy
And at least a bit of love
If not from Him directly
From my fellow man

I walk with careless sightless eyes
My ears unhearing
But for the sound
Of my own footsteps
The in and out of my breath
My heartbeat
The rushing of my blood
Away from it then back again

Forever searching
Hoping
I will know it when I see it
If I ever do

Why have you sold yourself?
Why have you given up on me?
In the age of your passion
At the time of your prosperity

The grace and purity of your youth
Has been forgotten
But not by me
And it never will
Let others forget
Your beauty
Your spotless soul

But you resigned all that
No one took them away
You gave them up
For the power of the flesh
In the name of corporeal survival
But it came at a cost

You gave away a gift from God
Something you had from birth
That was yours for free
But you need not have
Given up a thing
Lit up as you were
With the light of divinity
You sparkled and shined
With the glitter
Of a young goddess's pride

But you aspired to the mean
The air at the heights we lived
Too thin
To easily breathe

Voluntarily degraded
Easier to live among
People you were higher than
You've grown insolent
And bold

Basking in the adoration
Of the average man
Gaining favor with the money-men
Like a prostitute
Eager for the pleasure
She resisted for so long
When you lived for a higher purpose

Though not a babe
Still young enough
To enjoy some times of splendor
But you justified yourself in blood
By standing with those
Responsible for shedding it

Was your love for me
Some kind of fucking joke?

Once chaste and humble
With your beauty
An angel on Earth
You opted out of all you were
Simply to blend in
To be one of the majority
Sacrificing greatness
To be ordinary

You think you've won
But you have really lost
And when you lost
I did too

Fooled
Puffed up
By the approbation of
Those you were so much higher than
A major leaguer
Opting to play in the minor leagues
Content to be the biggest fish
In the smallest of seas
When you once were the one to be
In any sea you chose to swim in

Your fatal flaw?
You knew less about yourself
Than you should have
And less about me
Than you would

If
With all your gifts
You did not lack
The ability to see

If
you were brought up
With a different set of values
Your family is the cause of your imprisonment

If
You were less afraid
Of the freedom that was inside of you
Which
Truth be told
Cowered me

If
You could for a moment
See yourself
Through my loving eyes

You would have seen that you
Were born to fly
But they have put you in a cage
And you have stayed there willingly
The cage door left open

I guess you thought
You had to
For our four sons
Or perhaps
They were an excuse
For your co-option

2016 / 2019 / 2020 / 2021 / 2022

de RIGUEUR

Beaten and bruised
Beyond recognition
Somehow still standing
I am still strong
(Where it counts I mean)
They tried to break me
But all I did was bend

Unbroken
I remain a man
I've come to understand who I am
But I need not like it
I mean what it is I've come to know

There is a core to every man
Something we are born with
Impossible to change
But there's no limit placed
On what we can learn
With work
Make the man
We were born to be

That part of us
That will not change
Part of who we are

A well-lived life
Is one lived
From the lower to the higher

Not yet a ghost
My soul is still encumbered
Corporeally

Once the exception
Now the rule
The inmates run the asylums
Alan Bates
The King of Hearts
Kesey's Randall P. McMurphy

Art imitating life?
Life imitating Art ?
It really doesn't matter much

Normal now is crazy
Insanity de rigueur
A matter of survival
One must be insane to live
In this world as it is

There is a freedom
Being crazy
An exemption from the rules
Untethered
Free to soar
Unaccountable to anyone
Blameless
Before the law

Until they decide to confine you
They shoot you up
With all kinds of shit
They render you immobile
They mess with your capacity to think
To make you composed enough
To keep you in their power

They hate those unlike themselves
Terrified
Of anything or anyone
They don't understand

Allow me to come home to you
No strings attached
I'll not ask you
To love me again
I have no hope for that
But miracles do happen
And I'm way overdue

All I want to do is live with you
Live with you and wait
To be near you

To stand between you and hurt
To make up for the past
To keep you from suffering
Anymore

I would lay down my life
To serve you
Like a dog
Lay at your feet
Sit by your bed to watch you sleep

To prevent you from knowing more sorrow
Stand between you
And the evil in the world
To bring you joy and peace

To adore you
To hold you sacred
As befitting
The angel that you are

But it has never been simple for us
In my heart I can not leave you
I believe the same is so for you
A million small reasons why
Combining

Wishful thinking?
Perhaps

I would not bother you
If I was sure of what you really need
Even though
It would be worse than suicide
If you forever rejected me

I've not the strength to face it

I want to take your pain
Upon myself
I want to cry your tears for you
I know I've been the cause of most of them

For you I would be Hawkeye
The last of the Mohicans
Superman
Or some other superhero
For you the new Messiah

If only you would look at me again
The way you once did
With your green benotched
Kentucky Irish eyes
Full of love
Full of fire

Je t'aime beaucoup

2016 / 2019 / 2020 / 2021 / 2022

CPSIA information can be obtained
at www.ICGtesting.com
Printed in the USA
BVHW051050270423
663005BV00032B/112